The Trout Unlimited Book of
BASIC TROUT FISHING

The Trout Unlimited Book of

Introduction by

Robert L. Herbst
Executive Director
Trout Unlimited

Available from

National Sales Distributor
Charles E. Tuttle Co.
P.O. Box 410
Rutland, VT 05701

BASIC TROUT FISHING

Written and Illustrated by
Bill Cairns

Published by

Stone Wall Press, Inc.
1241 30th Street, N.W.
Washington, D.C. 20007

Cover design by Kim Hasten
Cover photo by R. Valentine Atkinson

Library of Congress Cataloging in Publication No. 82-50368
ISBN 0-913276-37-5

First Published September, 1980

Printed in the United States of America.
Third Printing - March, 1990

Acknowledgements

Special thanks for preparing Trout Unlimited
material should go to Craig Evans, Steven E.
Malone, and Thomas R. Pero.

Foreword

Trout Unlimited's book of *BASIC TROUT FISHING*, written and illustrated by Bill Cairns, was first published as part of *BACKPACKING FOR TROUT* (© Stone Wall Press, Inc., 1241 30th Street, NW, Washington, D.C., 1980—192 pages clothbound, $16.95). Bill, an avid angler well known to the fishing community, describes the foods trout eat, tells how to read water and gives important tips on the best methods to catch trout. He also explains how to select the correct fly and spinning tackle, how to decide what flies and lures to use, and how to fish different lakes, ponds and streams to catch more trout. You will also find tips from regional experts around the country. We hope this small book will help improve your trout fishing, as well as your enjoyment and appreciation of trout fishing.

The most important consideration is making sure the trout are there—and that is what *TROUT UNLIMITED* is all about.

About the Author

BILL CAIRNS was a founder of the world famous Orvis fly fishing school that originated in Manchester, Vermont. He has written *FLY CASTING WITH BILL CAIRNS* and *BACKPACKING FOR TROUT*. Bill has been a consultant to the tackle industry and manufactures his own rods.

CONTENTS

TROUT UNLIMITED

For each of us, trout fishing is an intensely personal experience—a chance, as Herbert Clark Hoover once said, to wash one's soul with pure air. There are times, of course, when your waders feel like hot tar paper in the sun, when the mosquitoes and blackflies outnumber the trout, and barricades of nettles guard the glassy pool where you want to cast your line. Yet there is a transformation as you step into a stream. Cold; gravel beneath your feet. The sounds of rushing water play on rubble, root and rapids, pierced at intervals by the scolding of a jay or the rattle of a kingfisher. Wet grass, moss and fern perfume the air. Suddenly, a trout rises. Forgotten are the long miles of hiking, the mosquitoes, all other concerns. You measure the distance and the cast . . . and wait for the familiar tug on your line—the moment when your rod comes springing to life, with the line tightening, rising and ratcheting off your reel.

Those of you who have never fished, but still love the out-of-doors where the senses come alive with the songs of birds, insects and wind, and the pulse quickens when you see a deer come to drink at the edge of a stream, know how important our water and fishery resources are. You can also appreciate what a valuable treasure is lost and how severely your enjoyment of the natural world is marred by pollution, over-development and other misuse of these resources.

That's why Trout Unlimited was formed: to preserve, protect and enhance the coldwater fishery of North America so that you and I—and all future generations—will have clean, clear water to enjoy and fish.

Trout Unlimited Philosophy

We believe that trout and salmon fishing isn't just fishing for trout and salmon. It's fishing for sport rather than for food, where the true enjoyment of the sport lies in the challenge, the lore and the battle of wits, not necessarily the full creel.

1

It's the feeling of satisfaction that comes from limiting your kill instead of killing your limit. It's communing with nature where the chief reward is a refreshed body and a contented soul, where a license is a permit to use—not abuse—to enjoy—not destroy our coldwater fishery. It's subscribing to the proposition that what's good for the trout and salmon is good for fishermen and that managing trout and salmon for themselves rather than for the fishermen is fundamental to the solution of our trout and salmon problems. It's appreciating our fishery resource, respecting fellow anglers and giving serious thought to tomorrow.

The History of Trout Unlimited

Trout Unlimited (TU) was the idea of George W. Mason, a foresighted man who died before he could see his idea become a reality. Born in a South Dakota sod hut to homesteader parents, George Mason, at the age of 43 became the president and chairman of the board of Nash-Kelvinator Corporation (which would later become American Motors). He lived in Michigan, and spent nearly every weekend in the marshes across the Detroit River waterfowl hunting or on the Au Sable River trout fishing. He was an avid waterfowl hunter and helped found Ducks Unlimited, serving as its treasurer until his death. But in the spring and summer, fishing the Au Sable was his love. For eighteen years he spent all the time he could on the South Branch, often fishing from Friday evening right through Sunday night. During the *Hexagenia* hatch, he was on the river daily, flying to his own small airstrip after work, fishing until midnight, breakfasting on the river and flying back to be in his Detroit office by nine or ten. His friend, George Griffith, spent many hours with him, and together they frequently discussed the need for an organization that would let people know how valuable trout resources are—a "Trout Unlimited" similar in concept to Ducks Unlimited.

When George Mason died in 1954, he deeded his entire Au Sable holding—ten miles of the river he had known and loved—to the State of Michigan. But his bigger legacy was his idea: Trout Unlimited.

George Griffith followed up on the idea, and in the summer of 1959, fifteen anglers met at his riverside home to discuss the need for an organization that would focus on trout—what kind of habitat they have and need—rather than on just their harvest. Ducks Unlimited had been successful in increasing waterfowl populations. So why not a "Trout Unlimited"? The name stuck, and plans were mapped out at this first meeting to form the organization.

One of the anglers present at the meeting—Art Neumann—immediately went out and signed up members. But it wasn't until later, on September 5, 1959, at a meeting in the American Legion Hall at Grayling, Michigan, that Trout Unlimited was formally organized. Dr. Casey Westell, Jr. was selected TU's first president and Art Neumann was elected vice president. Later, Neumann would become TU's first executive director.

In the beginning the fledgling organization concerned itself only with Michigan. Its leaders were aggressive, working to save trout fishing by organizing, publicizing and discussing the problem with anyone who would listen. They based their cause on a simple principle: what's good for the trout is good for the trout fishermen. The TU philosophy spread quickly. Anglers, tired of watching their fishing deteriorate, joined ranks. A nationwide movement to improve trout fishing was underway. By the late 1960s TU had several thousand members throughout sixteen states and the District of Columbia.

National recognition was gained for the programs, projects and litigation initiated by TU chapters. Many dedicated people, including George Griffith, Martin Bovey, Elliott Donnelley, Bob Evenson and Otto Teller nurtured the growing organization and built the broad, grassroots support that would make Trout Unlimited the largest, most active conservation organization dedicated to the coldwater fishery in America.

Now, well over two decades later, TU has grown to over 67,000 members with affiliates in Canada and New Zealand. TU's principal goal continues to be the protection and, where needed, the restoration of the coldwater trout environment. But TU's job has just begun . . .

Trout Unlimited in Action

To survive, trout and salmon must have cold, clear water. In fact, it was Otto Teller, a past TU president, who said, ". . . a healthy trout fishery is one sign of a well-managed stream environment. However, if the water becomes polluted and clogged with elements that destroy the clean water environment, the trout will die."

This is why Trout Unlimited members in more than 490 chapters across the country spend much of their free time in stream surveillance activities—constantly monitoring water quality in the streams, rivers and lakes—to observe the first signs of trouble. But far too often, surveillance alone is not enough.

Take Virginia, for example. Anglers appeared powerless during the 1960s and 1970s in the face of wholesale channelization that had turned more than 800 miles of the state's best trout streams into straight, fishless ditches. The Virginia Council of Trout Unlimited, however, launched a statewide campaign to focus public attention on the issue. Working with state officials, TU was able to halt this destruction by the U.S. Soil Conservation Service and others. In another noteworthy accomplishment, TU's Shenandoah Valley Chapter, working with the Virginia Department of Highways and Transportation, was able to preserve and enhance the trout fishery in Simpson Creek despite construction of a major highway through the area.

In Montana, Trout Unlimited helped lead the effort to keep the Yellowstone River flowing wild and undammed for 600 miles across the state. The upper third of the river is known worldwide as blue ribbon trout water. It is also the section dam builders proposed to flood behind Allenspur

Dam. Working with the Montana Department of Fish, Wildlife and Parks, the Montana Council of Trout Unlimited helped secure a historic decision by the state's Board of Natural Resources that designates free-flowing water in a river as a beneficial use. Montana officials called TU's support "crucial" in the year-and-a-half long court proceedings that led to the victory. What's more, the decision not only keeps the Yellowstone free-flowing, but sets an important precedent for water use throughout the West.

In New York State, New York City's water supply was the issue. For decades, erratic water releases from the city's upstate reservoirs had given the city a virtual stranglehold on the historic Catskill Mountains trout streams. Whole sections of the river frequently went dry in the summertime, often becoming so shallow that the water temperature would rise from 60° to 90°F. and killing thousands of trout. Art Flick, well-known fly-tier and angler, along with other members of the Catskill Mountains Chapter of Trout Unlimited, protested this poor water release policy to the U.S. Army Corps of Engineers with some success. Further action soon became necessary. Trout Unlimited joined with the Federation of Fly Fishers and other groups to form The Catskill Waters Coalition. Together, they successfully fought for legislation in 1976 to provide adequate stream flows to maintain trout and other aquatic organisms and to give the New York State Department of Environmental Conservation authority to control the water releases. The result: since 1977 there have been no more dry streambeds or high water temperatures. Esopus Creek, along with the Neversink and Delaware Rivers, beneficiaries of the planned water release, quickly returned to prominence among the best trout streams in the East—with no adverse effect on New York's water supply.

A Colorado "poster campaign" succeeded after the Ferdinand-Hayden Chapter of Trout Unlimited had watched improperly-treated sewage pour into the Roaring Fork River from the City of Aspen despite petitions and hearings with the health department. Even though a new sewage treatment plant was planned for the city, the Roaring Fork fishery would probably have disappeared before its projected completion date. In an effort to prevent this, signs reading "Fish taken from the Roaring Fork unfit for human consumption" began appearing along the river. Soon Aspen's new sewage plant was in full operation, well ahead of schedule. Thus a significant fishery was saved.

Elsewhere in the state, the Boulder Flycasters Chapter of TU successfully rehabilitated several channelized sections of Boulder Creek, which flows through the town of the same name. This was a long-term project, involving many individuals, businesses and agencies. It included stream surveys, publicity campaigns, pollution control efforts, adequate streamflow attainment, stream habitat improvement and trout stocking. The success of these efforts was so impressive that similar projects have been planned for other degraded streams in the area.

A newly-formed New Jersey TU chapter in Sparta went to bat with the help of many other chapters against the Tocks Island Dam and Reservoir proposal—a fight that would take ten years to resolve. The proposal, which called for impounding the Delaware River upstream of the famous Water Gap, would have backed water thirty-five miles upstream to Port Jervis, New York—ostensibly to provide power, flood control and recreation. As a result, numerous trout streams in northern New Jersey and the Pocono Mountains of Pennsylvania would have been flooded along with acres of forests, farmlands and wildlife habitat. TU members believed the project would be a boondoggle that would die of its own accord if its deficiencies were exposed to the public. TU chapters called upon the Washington office of Trout Unlimited to help build the case. After documenting objections to the project, the Sparta chapter arranged speaking engagements, pressed its case through the media and contacted Congressmen, state representatives and the Governor. As a result, the chairman of the President's Council on Environmental Quality ordered a halt to the project pending a complete environmental and economic review. In 1979, TU Executive Director Robert Herbst, then Assistant Secretary of the Interior, testified before Congress on behalf of the Carter Administration to deauthorize the project. Shortly afterwards, Congress passed the necessary legislation to halt the proposal and end its immediate threat to New Jersey and Pennsylvania trout streams.

In Washington State where dams and pollution have decimated many of the Northwest's once great runs of salmon and steelhead, Trout Unlimited has been working to prevent additional damage and re-establish runs of these great fish. In Bellingham, for instance, Trout Unlimited's Whatcom Chapter converted an old sewage treatment plant into rearing ponds for salmon and steelhead, and released over 100,000 fry into Whatcom Creek, where steelhead had been absent for several decades. The project was so impressive that the City of Bellingham used the sewage-plant-turned-hatchery as a central theme in 1978, helping it win the National All-American Small Cities top award. Whatcom Creek was a winner too. Today it supports healthy runs of steelhead!

Trout Unlimited's Northshore Chapter won national recognition for its work in building a rearing pond to raise steelhead and release them into Washington State's Skykomish River. This project, which has recently been expanded and made permanent, involves annual flooding of a farmer's field on Barr Creek, a tributary to the Skykomish. As a result of the farmer's cooperation, a starter grant from national TU and the Richard K. Mellon Foundation funding to TU National, and the volunteer efforts of TU members steelhead are returning to the Barr Creek area to spawn.

Over-fishing, habitat destruction and ill-advised plantings of hatchery fish all conspired to spell doom for the legendary Sol Duc River's wild steelhead. On Washington's wild and beautiful Olympic penninsula, members of Trout Unlimited's Fork's Chapter are successfully spearheading an effort to rebuild the declining runs. Each winter TU volunteers capture the few returning native steelhead by rod and reel. The finest and largest specimens are carefully kept alive for artifical spawning months later. The

5

fry are then raised to smolt size and released back into the Sol Duc. TU's Sol Duc project has become a model for dozens of similar native steelhead enhancement projects throughout the Northwest.

In the Seattle metropolitan area, the Green-Duwamish River has consistently ranked among the top salmon and steelhead producing rivers draining into Puget Sound. But its wild runs of fish were in jeopardy when the city of Tacoma began illegal construction of a pipeline from the river's headwaters. Tacoma sought quietly to double the quantity of water it was taking from the Green—reducing the streams flow to a virtual trickle for several months a year. Trout Unlimited's South King County Chapter blew the whistle, demanding that proper permits be obtained for this additional withdrawal. Today, a pending court decision looks promising for the Green-Duwamish and its wild salmon and steelhead.

In Massachusetts, TU's Southeastern Massachusetts Chapter invested more than six thousand hours of volunteer stream improvement work over a four year period to resore the wild trout fishery in the Quashnet River, a small, coastal stream on Cape Cod that had been damaged by construction of a dam and millpond in the mid-1800s and extensive cranberry farming throughout the first half of this century. The success of this project won recognition from Massachusetts Governor Edward J. King and the U.S. Department of the Interior, who together presented the chapter with the Heritage Conservation and Recreation Service Achievement Award—the highest honor given by the department to recognize important contributions by individuals and organizations in preserving America's natural resources.

More than three years were spent by Michigan's Leon P. Martuch Chapter restoring sections of the Tobacco and Cedar Rivers. Erosion, headwater impoundments, decaying instream structures and a massive fish kill, caused by whirling disease and the poisons used by the state to combat disease, decimated the trout populations. The chapter completed several stream improvement projects, stocked some areas with trout and recently purchased a fishing refuge for research and educational purposes. The tract was named in honor of Leon P. Martuch, a longtime member and founder of Scientific Anglers.

In Pennsylvania, TU's Forbes Trail Chapter worked hand-in-hand with the Pennsylvania Fish Commission, the local Army Reserve and CETA workers to rebuild Loyalhanna Creek after highway construction and massive flooding from Hurricane Agnes turned the downstream portion into a wide, fishless streambed. After thousands of tons of fill and stone, numerous deflectors and several years of work, Loyalhanna is once again a productive trout stream.

During its first ten years of existence, the Blair County TU Chapter struggled to end the pollution of a local trout stream, Halter Creek, by a large paper company. The chapter publicized the problem, worked to classify the stream as a coldwater fishery and testified in the face of strong opposition as to the true condition of the stream at several hearings. Their perseverance paid off in 1979 when the paper company agreed to cooperate in improving the stream. With their combined efforts and assistance from the Pensylvania Fish Commission, a large section of Halter Creek was cleaned up and stream improvement devices were installed. The following year the company signed a consent agreement to reduce its effluent and thermal pollution to acceptable levels.

TU's North Bay Chapter in California is working with a grant from the state and National TU's Operation Restore funds to complete work started in 1980, removing obstructions from Corte Madera Creek. These obstructions and dilapidated fishways have prevented runs of steelhead and salmon from entering the stream from San Francisco Bay for several decades.

Reports of Trout Unlimited's success continue to come in from around the country—from Utah, where TU's leadership helped save four trout streams from complete dewatering by the Central Utah Project; from New Mexico, where TU's participation in a legal suit helped save the San Juan River; from Wisconsin, where TU members studied and publicized the negative impacts of heavy population concentrations of beaver along trout streams; from New England, where TU has played a key role in the Atlantic salmon restoration project provided a model for better management of the state's wild trout streams; and from Maryland, where TU helped negotiate an historic arrangement to prohibit use of chlorine in treated sewage effluent entering natural trout waters.

Throughout North America and New Zealand, TU chapters continue their work—restoring lakes and streams that have been so adversely affected by erosion, siltation and pollution that trout and salmon can no longer survive in them; bringing back trout and salmon to rivers that are devoid of these fish because of dams and other obstructions; and protecting lakes, ponds and streams that are still healthy from the ravages of those who, by either ignorance or design, would destroy one of our greatest resources . . . and *your* fishing.

Trout Unlimited Today

Today, TU spans the United States, Canada, France, Spain and New Zealand, with affiliates in the U.S.S.R., China and Yugoslavia. Over 67,000 members are in 490 chapters under the umbrella of 30 state councils, all coordinated by the TU national office in Vienna, Virginia.

National Trout Unlimited is a leadership body which sets the agenda for TU programs nationwide and provides the necessary direction and support through its local chapters to get coldwater-related jobs done. Only through broad, grassroots support and action can we preserve our fisheries resource. To this end, Trout Unlimited is organized into national, regional, state and local units.

The heart of Trout Unlimited is its active and soundly-organized chapters. These local chapters give concerned anglers the opportunity to become directly involved in projects designed to benefit trout and salmon. They also provide the opportunity for people to learn how and where to fish, including fly-tying and casting demonstrations, to participate in sporting events and youth-oriented activities, and to enjoy the companionship of other anglers and conservationists working together to protect and enhance one of America's most priceless heritages: the coldwater fishery. Twelve members, including officers, and official chapter name and adopted bylaws are required to form a chapter. In addition to their formal organization, successful chapters use valuable volunteer time, talents and resources of members to sponsor educational programs and research, write and publish fishing information, maintain surveillance on nearby lakes and streams, follow through on local environmental issues and assist state and federal agencies in conducting stream surveys, scientific research, and other fish management projects.

Trout Unlimited's state councils coordinate chapter activities and projects within a state or region. They provide a vehicle for communication between local chapters, states and the national organization via representatives elected to TU's National Board of Directors. They also form new chapters, build TU membership and speak as a unified voice for anglers on state legislative and fisheries matters.

At the national level, TU produces and distributes educational films and printed materials, and publishes *TROUT* magazine and *ACTION LINE* newspaper, which contain articles on important fishing and conservation issues. The national office works with Congress and federal agencies for the protection and wise management of America's fishing waters; sponsors national symposiums on issues such as acid rain, water pollution and wild trout management; funds fisheries reseach; presents testimony on water resource issues; handles all daily business, including TU's membership and financial management; and provides fund raising, staffing and technical expertise that would otherwise not be available to local groups acting alone.

The business, property and affairs of Trout Unlimited are the responsibilities of the National Board of Directors, comprised of sixty-four elected members, who decide on organizational actions and policies at semi-annual meetings in March and August.

The responsibility of carrying out these decisions rests with TU's Executive Committee, which meets four times each year and is comprised of the President, First Vice-President, six Regional Vice-Presidents, Secretary-Treasurer, Chairman of the Board, and five Department Chairmen.

Trout Unlimited also has a Scientific Advisory Board to provide professional fisheries-related expertise to the organization, and a special Advisory Board comprised of members active in the conservation field who also contribute their knowledge to Trout Unlimited.

TU's funding comes from membership dues, special projects, contributions and grants from corporations and foundations. Because Trout Unlimited is a nonprofit, conservation organization with a 501(c)3 tax-deductible designation from the Internal Revenue Service, all private contributions and grants to the organization are tax-deductible.

Trout Unlimited Tomorrow

Environmental quality doesn't just happen. Considerable care and skill are required to develop community awareness of the impact of human activities on living natural systems. For example, industrial production necessary for a thriving national economy sometimes produces acid rain that changes the pH balance of watercourses in the Northeast and many other parts of the continent, making them unfit for most aquatic life. Hundreds of lakes are dead, and perhaps thousands more are dying. With the deterioration of these lakes, the quality of life in entire regions of the continent is severely diminished. Additionally, improperly-treated sewage and other effluents change the chemistry of receiving streams, affecting the kinds of fish and other life that can live in and around those waters. Our quality of life is diminished when this occurs. Dams across streams radically alter aquatic habitat. When a coastal stream is blocked, salmon cannot return to their natural spawning areas. Atlantic salmon once teemed in the coastal rivers of the eastern United States; now only remnants of the wild stocks remain. The great anadromous fish streams of the West Coast and the Pacific Northwest are also in jeopardy because of short-sighted policy decisions. The basic error is rapid construction of huge, power-generating dams to solve one social need but which fails to recognize the basic survival needs of the trout and salmon runs which are socially critical to an entire region.

The members of Trout Unlimited understand that a quality habitat produces good fishing. So when TU members set out to maintain and enhance habitat for trout and salmon, they are involved in *much more* than simply supplying fish for the angler. They are working to clean up pollution from industrial plants, improve waste-water treatment and promote policies that support sound water-quality management. Furthermore, TU chapters are involved in streambank and streambed restoration to improve aquatic habitat.

Trout Unlimited understands that efforts to protect fish habitat begin far from the streambank, far from the sparkling, living bright water. Environmental quality begins with strong leadership by those with an awareness of the delicate balance of natural, living systems. It continues right through to the thousands of volunteers in hundreds of TU chapters who roll up their sleeves for on-the-ground projects; work with the media; testify before agencies, legislative bodies and courts; sponsor seminars; publish resource material; participate in educational programs and, on occasion, find time to fish.

Their job is far from done. Let's take a look at two of the most pressing current problems and challenges . . .

Acid Rain

One of the growing problems facing our fishery today is acid precipitation or deposition, commonly referred to as acid rain. This is caused by the conversion of sulfur and nitrogen oxides in the upper atmosphere into sulfuric and nitric acids. The acids are transported to earth in rain and snow and as dry fallout.

The major sources of sulfur oxides are coal-burning power plants and industrial boilers. Nitrogen oxides come primarily from automobiles and coal-fired boilers. In 1980, polluters in North America alone discharged 35 million tons of sulfur oxides and 24.5 million tons of nitrogen oxides into the air. By the year 2000, these discharges are expected to increase to 36.6 million tons of sulfur oxides and 31.9 million tons of nitrogen oxides annually if action is not taken to reduce emissions.

The ways in which acid rain affects fish and aquatic food chains are extremely complex. Some aspects of the effects are not thoroughly understood, but this much is known for sure: acid rain kills fish and causes their extirpation from susceptible lakes and streams, usually through reproductive failure. Acid rain also causes major changes in aquatic food systems, although there is no current evidence that fish die from starvation.

While the long-term acidification of lakes and streams is a serious problem, the most dramatic impacts on fish come from what scientists call acid snowmelt and rainfall shock. During spring snowmelt or when highly acidic rain falls on already saturated ground the pH of streams and lakes can drop so low that fish die. During these critical periods acid rain causes leaching of heavy metals from the soil and bedrock. These metals, primarily aluminum but also mercury, cadmium and lead, in turn become more toxic in acid water.

Fish kills caused directly by acid rain have been documented in the United States' Adirondack Mountains, Scandinavia and Canada. The acids, working alone or in combination with leached metals, cause the fishes' gills to become covered with mucus. The fish die from suffocation.

More commonly, however, the fish disappear from acidified lakes and streams because of reproductive failure. Acidic water can inhibit development of reproductive organs and reduce egg production and sperm viability in some species of fish. In other species it kills the very sensitive embryos and fry. Among the most susceptible game species are largemouth bass and walleyes, followed by rainbow trout, lake trout, brown trout, northern pike, rock bass, Atlantic salmon and brook trout.

Acid rain is not a new phenomenon. This used to be a local problem in areas downwind of power plants and other industries. But tall smokestacks now send the pollution high into the atmosphere which in turn causes a problem for much of North America. The rain falling over the Eastern United States and neighboring areas of Canada is 10 to 100 times more acidic than normal. The rainfall from some storms is 1,000 times more acidic.

Trout Unlimited has identified acid rain as its number one national resource priority. A nationwide campaign is underway to educate the anglers of America and the general public to the danger posed by this growing environmental tragedy. National TU has produced special acid rain slide presentations, published educational brochures, and sponsored scientific conferences to seek a better understanding of, and solutions to, this problem. But TU realizes that much more needs to be done. We have only taken the first step.

Hydropower

Another emerging issue is the rapidly increasing development of small-scale hydropower, especially the use of moving water to turn turbines that produce electrical power. The direct use of water as a power source is not a new concept, as evidenced by the gristmills of colonial times. However, modern hydropower facilities can be quite complex and cause an array of environmental problems for our fisheries. Dams are often used to control the flow of water to generate electricity. Dams without fish ladders obstruct fish passage and drastically alter the upstream characteristics of the river and stream ecology. Spent water released downstream causes changes in water level, flow, temperature and quality.

Construction of hydropower projects causes disruption of the aquatic ecosystem and may present turbidity problems downstream of the site. Once a dam is in place, upstream fish migration is virtually eliminated unless some type of fish passage facility is included. Any fry or other fish traveling downstream must either pass over the dam or through the turbines via the release water. Those that survive are often so stressed by the experience that they become easy prey for birds and other aquatic predators. Even the water below the dam, if supersaturated with nitrogen, can additionally cause fish mortality by producing gas bubble disease.

Water impounded behind the dam will inundate adjacent riparian habitat and increase the water surface, which can increase water temperatures as a larger volume of water is warmed by the sun. This lake-type habitat may be unsuitable for stream-dwelling trout and other riverine fish. The water may stratify, with a warm, nutrient-poor environment at the surface and heavily-sedimented substrates that inhibit trout and salmon reproduction.

The downstream area below the dam can also be greatly affected by the power plant's operation. A major problem is the variation in water level and flow that can occur due to erratic water releases. Spawning areas can be dramatically altered as water is released, or may be left exposed as water is withheld or pumped into storage. The temperature of the released water is often much different from that of the receiving stream. Warm impoundment water entering a cold trout stream can seriously stress the fish. When large volumes of water are released they may scour the downstream habitat and cause turbidity problems, suffocating the fish or forcing them to emigrate.

Not all hydropower development has to create these problems. Hydropower facilities at existing dams will usually have little additional effect on fishery resources, though some type of mitigation may be needed in order to restore or enhance fish populations. New hydropower development and major modifications in existing structures must be carefully planned and constructed to protect local fisheries. Fish passage facilities, guaranteed instream flow rates and careful monitoring of the hydropower operation can help preserve our valuable trout and salmon resources.

Both of these issues, acid rain and hydropower development, present challenges to our natural resources. Our task for the future is to recapture and rekindle our commitment to the legacy left us by our founders. This obligation is written in the *Environmental Ethic,* which decrees that every man is the keeper of his brother; and that no man has the right to corrupt the heritage of all men. One of our greatest heritages and traditions is trout, salmon and steelhead fishing.

We Need You!

If you are not yet a member of TU let me ask you now to join Trout Unlimited, and help preserve for your own children and grandchildren the sport and challenge of trout fishing you enjoy so much today. Through sound management and concerted action, trout, salmon and steelhead fishing—one of America's priceless heritages—will continue to be enjoyed for many generations to come. But we need your help to make it happen. At the back of this book are TU membership blanks so that you, your family and your friends can join TU and join the efforts to preserve our fisheries.

Because You Are Important to TU

Without your active concern the joys of nature as we now know them will be lost forever. We have to work hard to maintain and improve the environment.

The source of much of our food, raw materials and recreation depends upon our productive croplands, forests, grasslands and fisheries. But these life-sustaining systems are constantly being burdened by the needs of increasing numbers of people.

We have the power to destroy or improve our environment.

Like me, you may find yourself wrestling with your own desires for luxury items that neither the economy nor the environment can support. How far are we prepared to go, as a nation, in accomodating both development and preservation? How far are we prepared to go in our own *private* lives to express our *public* environmental ethic?

This is not a quiz. I throw out these questions only to highlight some of the decisions we are now making, as a nation. But the answers will appear later, *written on the face of our land and water—stamped on the quality of our lives.*

Every age must make its own pact with destiny: its high moral purpose must be shaped in terms of the needs of THAT age. The urgency of this age is to face up to the end of abundance, to explore the common ground where men and women of good sense and good will can work out ways of living that make us proud to be human.

If we adopt the practice of caring for our environment, I am optimistic about our future.

The philosophy on safeguarding nature that I like best and believe in most is found in the words of Richard Doer, a departed friend and conservation colleague from Minnesota:

> *"Your Creator has created all things necessary*
> *to sustain you and found them to be good.*
> *While you dwell among the mortals you may par-*
> *take.*
> *Use them wisely and judiciously.*
> *Guard them closely, squander them not.*
> *For if you are untrue to this sacred trust,*
> *mankind will not be perpetuated—but will*
> *perish from this earth."*

This is our charge. As a member of Trout Unlimited, *you* can make a difference. You can make a contribution toward building our world into a better place in which we all can live.

Robert L. Herbst
Executive Director
Trout Unlimited
501 Church St. N.E.
Vienna, Va, 22180

January, 1990

2.

TROUT SENSES

In spite of a modest ranking on the evolutionary scale, trout are well-suited to their specialized environment and possess a number of keen sensory receptors which respond to a variety of impressions. Many anglers feel they are an ideal quarry; shy, cautious, and demanding of an angler's good effort if there is to be a degree of consistency in their capture.

The hearing of trout is an unusually versatile sensory system that is essential to their feeding and survival. This is a two part system, and yes, trout have ears (although they are internal, rather than external). Their hearing is aided by a connection between the swim bladder and the inner ear. Essentially the swim bladder is a membrane-enclosed chamber capable of serving as an underwater amplifier, microphone and resonating chamber. The bladder notices vibration which is magnified and transmitted to the inner ear. Trout also have lateral line sensitivity to vibration. The lateral line begins on the head as a canallike network. Behind the head canals join and form the true lateral line extending towards the tail. The two systems are complementary to the extent that the lateral line detects primarily near-field vibrations and the inner ear system is alert to more distant sounds. The systems are so sensitive that a nearby baitfish, worm or nymph may be detected without being seen. The systems hear various low frequency, auditory stimuli from about ten to fifteen cycles per second to some 10,000 cycles per second. In a comparative sense, the average human hears in the ranges of about twenty to 20,000 cycles per second.

Sound travels underwater at about one mile per second, a rate about five times the speed of travel in the air. Additionally, sound intensity is not decreased nearly so much as in the air, since water is an excellent sound wave conductor. Despite this, our talking back and forth above the surface will not alarm the trout to our presence. These air borne sounds are not easily transmitted into the water. The surface is a very effective barrier to most air borne sound formations. Although talking will not alarm the trout to our presence, we can easily alert them in other ways. Any object in contact with the water will easily transmit warning vibrational echoes. The angler should wade carefully, especially in quiet waters, and tread softly along bordering stream banks. In turbulent waters our presence may be muted by the sounds of the stream itself as it tumbles and cascades. For reasons of secure footing and personal safety, we should be cautious and slow moving in the rapids.

The olfactory senses are also well developed. Two nostrils are arranged as U-shaped tubes in the snout of the fish. Water passing through the tubes flows over highly sensitive nerve endings. This system is so sensitive that it can detect some odors diluted into the incredible ratios of parts per billion. It can, for instance, detect the odor of other nearby fish and make distinctions between them. A crippled bait fish giving off an alarm substance as its distress may be checked out quickly in the hope of obtaining an easy meal. Perhaps we should confirm the suspected: Sensory systems work in conjunction with one another. Our theoretically crippled, fluttering bait fish may be detected by odor, by sight, or it may be detected through vibrational echoes set up by its struggles. The underlying point remains the same: Trout are keenly aware of what is happening around them.

Some of the various odors that have been found to deter or frighten trout include human skin, insect repellents, and various petroleum-based products. In an attempt to counteract these considerations, there are various scents offered by some manufacturers for application to flies and lures. Whether these offerings actually have the ability to attract trout or simply achieve an effect of masking human odors is a consideration I've never analyzed. However, given the olfactory sensitivity of the trout plus the demonstrated success of chumming, stink baits, etc. for other species, it is reasonable to assume that scent could be an attractor element in many circumstances, especially in turbid waters when normal keen vision of the trout is greatly hampered. I recall a conversation over a Colorado campfire when one of the group smeared bacon fat over his Marabou Muddler, assuring me, "It works like a charm."

There is an obvious relationship between odor discrimination and taste. Trout have taste buds on the inside of their mouths. Unfortunately, some taste buds exist outside the mouth as well. This means a trout can actually taste something without taking it into its mouth. The occasional gentle bump to a fly or lure may indicate an attempt to taste the object before actually striking.

Vision is another extremely important sensory capacity, and their ability to accurately define and intercept drifting nymphs and flies is reliable proof of their capabilities.

In spite of the obvious environmental differences, the lidless eye of the trout is surprisingly like our own basic structure. The retina's sensor lining includes both rods and cones. Rods permit light-sensing functions in marginal and very low level illuminations, while the cones are color sensitive and function in ordinary daylight levels. As the light levels diminish into darkness the rod cells

16

are utilized, permitting the trout to still see well, especially in terms of size and silhouette. They appear to retain a degree of tonal value discrimination at night even if color vision is absent. Many hatches occur in the darkness and are silhouetted against the night sky. The most successful anglers attempt to reasonably suggest the size, shape, and tonal values of the natural insect. If the essential values are light in color, the artificial should also be light in color; if dark values predominate, the artificial should be correspondingly dark. Imitative precision may not be required but reasonable approximation is still advantageous. Well in advance of dawn the cones begin extending in anticipation of daylight, and the trout evidences excellent abilities in the areas of color perception and shape discrimination.

Since water is a lesser conductor of light than air, the trout have little need for long range vision and are primarily nearsighted. As their eyes are placed on the sides of the head they have a very wide field of sight and they are able to use their eyes independently or together.

Used independently, each eye is able to scan an area of about 180°. When both eyes are focused on a subject, the field of view is rather narrow. Most authorities indicate 45° as the likely field of view. Because of the location of their eyes, trout have a small blind spot directly below and behind themselves.

Their ability to see above the surface is affected by and related to the physical properties of light. As light rays pass from the air to the water they are bent or refracted. The degree of refraction is proportional to the angle at which the light rays strike the surface. Light rays that are perpendicular to the surface are not bent, while those rays entering nearly parallel to the surface are refracted at an angle of 48.5°. Because light may enter the surface from all directions, the trout can see all objects above the surface. However light rays are bent as they enter the water and funnel into a conelike shape having an apical angle of 97°. The narrow base of the cone leads up to the window or circular hole in the surface. The trout's view through the window shows objects in the center area of the window most clearly, while items at the edges of the window are blurred and compressed. Their single view to the outside world is through this window. The remainder of the underside of the surface becomes mirrorlike, bouncing back the light and forming an image of the bottom.

Close approaches to visible trout, especially in slow flowing or calm, clear water are best accomplished by crouching to remain low, towards the edges of the window where any image seen by the trout may be indistinct and compressed. In addition to bending low, side arm casts are often the most advantageous offering with close approaches. Kneeling and crawling tactics can be helpful, and bank-bound anglers should take advantage of boulders, brush, and other cover to break up and confuse their outlines.

The exact size of the trout's window varies with the depth of the fish. At about six inches beneath the surface the window is approximately a foot. The fish most interested in near-surface and surface activity often hold some six to eighteen inches beneath the surface with their attention concentrated upward. Any deep-lying fish have a proportionately larger window to the world but they are more apt to be concentrating their attention on deep lying or deep drifting food forms.

Anglers often question why a trout should take an artifical fly at all, especially when the hook appendage is so obvious. It is a question of vexing specificity. Although we cannot know the total answer, we gain partial insight by realizing that although their eyes detect color, size, form, motion perception and contrast, the eyes of the trout provide a comparatively lesser capacity for exact detail. Their ability to see sharply is best when an object is at right angles to their eyes. They sacrifice some detail for depth perception enhancement when they look straight ahead and snap at a fly. In effect, a sense of familiar, recognizable "insectness" at this critical moment, rather than each specific detail is what is being zeroed in on. The more important triggering mechanisms are size, shape or silhouette, color (though not necessarily exact shading) and movement, or equally important, lack of movement. Some of the swirling last minute refusals we experience may result from unusual behavioral characteristics.

A natural may fly will drift freely with the vargaries of an existing current while our artificial fly, attached to a leader, may become subject to unnatural motion or drag. Although drag is often anticipated or detected by the angler and compensated for, some movement is so subtle as to be invisible to the angler. The trout, just inches away, is the definitive judge of such things. Active insects fluttering or struggling on the surface film may be suggested by subtle twitches delivered through a sensitive rod hand. On a few occasions movement is advantageous even when the natural flies are drifting motionless. Such moments might occur when a hatch is particularly heavy and your offering is just one of thousands available. We experienced such moments in the Labrador interior when mayfly emergences on the shallow lakes were enormous. Brook trout to seven pounds were gulping in the naturals with abandon. It seemed pure chance that our single artificial could be found in the midst of such activity. When we began to skitter our offerings, the movement caught the eye of the heavy trout. They would move consistently to our gently twitched offerings.

In addition to behavior, and certainly as important on a day-to-day basis, are the size and silhouette of our offerings. They may be close enough to bring an investigative arousal but not quite close enough to finish the job. Matching size becomes increasingly important as the fly becomes smaller in size. A suggestively lifelike appearance becomes more important as the currents slow. In the slower flows the trout have infinitely more time to spiral up and inspect the drifting fly, for the current won't wash it rapidly away. In quick, turbulent flows a more reflexive attack is required as the potential food form would be quickly lost to the current. This strongly suggests that during emergence activity the angler pay more attention to size, shape, color and manner of movement in slow to medium currents than would be required in tumbling, cascading flows. Actually, if trout were capable of expressing emotion, we'd probably find these last minute refusals were as disappointing to them as they are to us (although we usually suspect otherwise). Their daily well-being is a constant battle between expended energy and the capture of an adequate food supply. They investigate, hoping to reinforce their initial impression of the correct "insectness" and behavior of our offerings.

In turbid, vision-hindered water, trout must depend heavily on their unusual lateral line sensitivity and sense of smell for much of their food location. Many anglers respond to such water conditions by selecting somewhat larger than normal flies in tonal values that enhance contrast. If fishing subsurface, which is the norm under such conditions, tinsel-ribbed flies reflect any available light values as the trout moves in close. Fly patterns such as the Muddler and, of course, various spin lures may set up vibrational echoes that stimulate lateral line sensitivity and aid in locating the offering in such discolored water conditions. Fishing the water more slowly and more thoroughly is also productive for any prey must be accurately located before the trout can strike. In milky waters that prevail on some limestone streams and snow-melt waters, as well as those coffee brown runoff waters, large dark flies are often employed for contrast enhancement.

In normal conditions of seasonal water levels and clear water, if you're stuck for a subsurface starting point, select a fly corresponding to the stream bottom values. Nature protects the otherwise defenseless nymphs and larva primarily through protective coloration. They usually blend in well with their surroundings. A dislodged or drifting nymph under these clear water conditions doesn't require contrast enhancement. The trout's eye is very sensitive to movement and they expect to see something appropriate to the locale.

The ability of trout to select is another, much discussed, consideration. Obviously the ability exists and is of great value to the well being of the trout. Over the long haul the trout is an opportunistic feeder, snapping at what is available within the confines of a rubble foundation and moving, liquid roof to his world. However, when an emergence of an insect species begins, there is an entirely different situation. Thousands of a similar species become available, all moving in a similar manner, all of a similar size, shape and appropriate color. The trout becomes quite specific in its feeding habit in order to make maximum utilization of this temporary abundance. By selecting a site in the flow where the current brings a constant drift line of insects, the trout is able to initiate and repeat a muscular movement of great efficiency, intercepting the drifting insect, then returning to precisely the same spot (by fixing a specific location on the retina) to lie in wait for another insect before repeating the same muscular pattern. This is certainly the most efficient way to utilize this transitory abundance.

The artifical offered at such a time should be of a similar size, silhouette, color and manner of movement as the natural. The best presentation is the natural drift line of the insects that the specific trout is intercepting. The trout certainly won't move a foot to one side to take your artifical when it is in the feeding rhythm of picking the naturals off overhead.

Selectivity is at once a strength and a potential Achilles heel for the angler.

All we have to do is put the right fly in the right place.

Many fertile waters have times when two, three, or more insect species are emerging simultaneously. It's critical to determine not only which insect your trout is taking, but the developmental state of the insect as well. Numerical abundance or relative ease of capture may be the influencing factors determining which stage and which insect the trout is feeding on. Careful observation of the hatch is most important. There may be a small, darkly colored species available in vast numbers which are difficult to see while you concentrate your imitative efforts on a more visible species which the trout are ignoring at the moment. Under difficult lighting conditions or on large streams, a small pair of binoculars can be surprisingly useful. You can visually locate and follow a particular fly to determine its fate. Later, when the specific hatches are over, some trout may begin to cruise, searching for any leftovers from the hatch, or they may show susceptibility to other offerings in an opportunistic manner.

In spite of their voracious feeding during specific hatches, they are often strangely cautious with the arrival of a new food form on the scene. Most hatches run their course in a week or ten days to be replaced by another species attaining numerical superiority. Yet there seems to be a recognition factor at work and an initial reluctance to change to the new insect form. On the upper section of a river that I fish regularly, the arrival of *Ephemerella dorothea* (locally Pale Evening Duns or Sulphurs) is well regarded and capable of providing good activity. Surprisingly, the first day or two that we notice some emergence activity, the trout ignore the little flies and prefer instead larger, darker, spinner patterns that have been the standard offerings for the past several evenings. By the third day the trout seem to have reconciled any early recognition problems and feed avidly on the buttery yellow little flies. On this same stream section we also see a few, but very few, *Ephemera varia* (locally: Yellow Drake) emerge. Trout in this section ignore them even though they are large and drift placidly for long distances on the slow-flowing current. We've often watched naturals drift a hundred yards or more through feeding trout and not be taken. Yet thirty miles downriver where the steam is considerably larger and population levels of *E. varia* are considerably higher, this is an eagerly awaited emergence. Large trout rise well to their appearance.

Still another consideration directly affecting the trout is water temperature. Since trout are cold-blooded, their body temperatures are those of the surrounding waters. This heat transfer process speeds up or slows down the metabolic processes. Consequently, water temperatures have a direct bearing on reproduction, feeding, growth and survival.

Their sensitivity to temperature changes is such that they are capable of detecting differences of less than half a degree. Such sensitivity has many applications. Sea run trout and salmon supplement their keen sense of smell when migrating along a thermal current enroute to distant feeding grounds or returning to their home rivers. It is also fundamental to their ability to locate spring holes, cold water seepages, and cooling tributaries in times of distressingly high water temperatures in the main body of water.

Angling results are often directly affected by water temperature. Trout will feed all year round; however, metabolic functions are greatly slowed in the cold water of winter. Food taken in may require four to five days or more to be fully digested, so the length of time between stomach refills is greatly lengthened.

As waters warm beyond comfortable limits, trout often seek out riffly or rapid areas, spring hole seepages, or cooling tributaries in search of higher oxygen contents and/or cooler temperatures.

As water temperatures rise, trout require more food more often, as their body processes are greatly accelerated. More energy is being used. They are increasingly active and digestive times are greatly shortened. Most authorities conclude that maximum trout growth occurs between 45° and 66° although trout can and do feed above and below these benchmarks.

Fly fishermen who have charted their results in relation to prevailing water temperatures tend to prefer a reasonably narrow range, from about 55° to 68°. At 68° and warmer the availability of insect activity to stimulate feeding seems to become more and more important. With warming temperatures it is much more difficult to simply pound up a trout by thoroughly covering the water. Additional stimulation in the form of insect activity greatly enhances the prospects of success at such times.

When waters warm above comfortable limits, the trout tend to search out rapid waters. If temperatures climb toward the mid seventies, they often concentrate in cool tributaries or spring hole seepages. At these temperatures trout may be distressed either because of water temperatures or insufficient oxygen contents in the water. During these periods you can often find cooler, more desirable temperatures upstream, near the stream source, or in various tributary streams. Trout gravitate toward cooler areas. Surprisingly large trout are sometimes found in such cool, sheltered areas. Some regions have cold water releases on rivers that have been impounded for water supply use or hydroelectric power generation. Water released to the rivers from the bottom of such impoundments flow cool and may exert an influence for several miles on the main stream.

Because of the direct relationships of temperature and trout activity, many anglers habitually carry a small stream thermometer. Move a reasonable distance into the stream, shade the thermometer from the direct sun, and hold it beneath the surface long enough for it to register a consistent reading. On ponds and lakes the same situation applies. Many anglers tie the thermometer to a length of monofilament or discarded fly line section so they can lower it deep in a search for spring holes or cold water seepages.

Throughout the most desirable temperature ranges, digestion may take twelve hours or less. A fish, well-fed late in the evening, may prowl for food towards dawn. Food taken in then is well digested by evening. Any daytime insect activity or availability can also trigger feeding responses, but there are usual feeding rhythms of early and late in the day throughout much of the season. As we've mentioned previously, trout see well during these periods of low level illumination and coincidentally feel more secure with regard to possible animal or bird predators. Dull overcast days or broken surfaces, distorted by current or wind, may also promote a greater than normal sense of security. In bright weather, when there is no insect activity to stimulate feeding responses or when temperatures are marginal, trout often retreat to cover beneath the mainstream currents, shadowy undercuts, boulders and the like. Here they may assimilate any food taken in, rest, minimize location indexing by various predators, and find a comfortable diffusion of light or shade.

Although there will always be unanswered and perhaps some unanswerable questions regarding trout behavior, all anglers can benefit from the reminder that we are dealing with a wary, well-adapted creature who is constantly alert to events around him. Any specifics of how well they can hear or see may be soon forgotten, but if we retain the overall impression of their capabilities it may help us slow down and be more careful in our approaches and presentations. Such considerations should prove bountiful over the long run.

3.

FOOD FORMS

Trout food forms of potential importance to the angler are many and varied, including insects of both aquatic and terrestrial origins. Additionally, there are various baitfish, true bugs, and crustaceans which assume varying degrees of local or seasonal importance and require imitative efforts.

Within the rather elastic framework of aquatic insects, the most prominent are mayflies, stoneflies, caddis flies and various midges. Terrestrials may also be represented variously, but the primary imitative problems lie with grasshoppers, crickets, beetles, leafhoppers, inchworms and ants. True bugs may include water boatmen and backswimmers. Scuds and sow bugs are abundant in many fertile waters and may require suggestion. Baitfish comprise another wide range of opportunity with sculpin, dace, shiners, chubs, darters and others, including immature trout, showing up in the diet of large trout.

Since we are treading a fundamental path, discussion will be limited to rather general characteristics and habits. There is an abundance of excellent literature available for additional reference in keeping with an individual's developing attitudes and interests.

The mayflies spend most of their life underwater in immature stages of their growth cycle. By contrast, the winged adult stages are brief, typically one to three days. The life cycle consists of four states: egg, nymph, dun (or sub imago), and spinner (or imago). The latter three stages are of angling significance. Because there is no pupal stage, the life cycle is referred to as incomplete metamorphosis.

The usual life span of most species is about a year with a few of the smaller species being multibrooded within the framework of a single season. These non-typical species may have a life cycle of two to three months. Some of the largest, burrowing mayflies may require three years to complete their span.

Typically, the newly emerged nymph is almost microscopic. Most, but not all, are vegetarian and consume the diatoms and other microscopic plant organisms and occasionally chew at the tissues of higher plants. The numphs are enormous contributors to the life of fresh waters by changing plant life materials into animal tissue which can then serve as food for larger, predatory insects and higher forms such as the trout. Rather rapid nymph growth occurs. To accommodate this growth, the nymphs moult (twenty or even thirty times in some species). During the moult the nymph splits the restraining nymphal shuck at the thorax and head and struggles free. The nymph is typically pale, almost transparent, and defenseless until the chitin hardens in its new skin and normal coloration is regained. The period between moults is termed an instar.

Anglers tend to categorize mayfly nymphs into four approximate classifications depending on their nymphal habits. These categories recognize and differentiate the various specific adaptations to the aquatic communities in which they are found.

BURROWERS are usually found along the banks or in quiet stream stretches and pools as well as at the bottom of ponds and lakes. They are able to dig in the silt and fine gravel materials with their flattened, shelflike heads, large mandibular tusks, and flattened front legs. They feature long plumose gills, situated around upon their back so they are not injured when digging or burrowing. These gills are in almost constant motion to keep a current of water flowing. These nymphs are comparatively large and are usually less than two inches below the substratum surface, but they have been found to depths of several inches. On occasion they may be noted above the stream water line where they have dug into the wet banks. Their long, sweeping tails are visible as they project from their burrows.

CLINGERS are tenacious, fast-water dwellers, whose forms are greatly flattened. In most species the gills are platelike, overlapping to form a ventral suction disc. Heads are wide and eyes are located at the top lateral edge. Normally these have a single year life cycle.

SWIMMERS Depending on the species, they enjoy a range of water types. Body shapes are similar in that they are slender and cylindrical. The lentic or calm-water species have heavily fringed tails that provide propulsion in swimming. They climb about vegetation, darting in and out of shelter and occasionally swimming out into open water areas with excellent agility. Generally the calm-water species are small to medium in size. The lotic or running-water species are larger, although similar in habit and agility. When at rest they face upstream.

CRAWLERS may be found in various water types, but medium currents harbor the greatest numbers. As a group they are slightly depressed in shape or ovoid in cross-sectional shapes, thin tailed, and the gills are often reduced in number and are dorsal in position. They are poor swimmers and tend to walk about in the debris and bottom rubble, or sit, silt covered.

In all cases, when the elapsed time for the species involved has passed and suitable water temperatures are attained, the nymphs stop both feeding and growing. Wing pads or cases darken, becoming virtually black in some cases. Emergence to the air is accomplished in various ways: some migrate to the shallows or crawl out on rocks; some escape the restraining nymphal shuck at the stream bottom or within a few inches of the surface, emerging through the surface film as adult duns. Most species swim or struggle to the surface where, with the aid of the surface tension, they complete their transformation to the dun.

Mayfly emergence activity generally begins when water temperatures reach the upper forties to fifty degrees for a period of two to three days. This early season activity is typically in the afternoon when waters are at their warmest. The duration for any single species is normally from a few days to about ten days.

Fortunately nature is repeatable to the extent that the same species will emerge about the same time each year. Climatic variables may exert an influ-

The mayfly dun exhibits an upright wing as opposed to the flattened wing of the adult stonefly or the tent wing shape of the caddis fly. Normally there is a second pair of wings of much reduced size—although this feature is lacking in a few species.

ence by a factor of a few days one way or another. But, on the whole, the repeatability is surprising.

Colorations of the mayfly duns are various, ranging through mostly subdued shadings: early season's greyish/brownish values, various olive shadings, tan to medium brownish, creamy yellow to ginger and dark brownish, to almost black. Body lengths are obviously variable with different species and encompass a typical range from about one-eight of an inch to about one and one half inches.

On leaving the water, the dun seeks the comparative safety of streamside foliage. Not all enemies have been left behind when he escapes the trout. Those swooping and darting swallows, waxwings, and other birds capitalize on the abundant availability as well. Resting on the underside of leaves, the dun does not feed. Mouth parts have atrophied and are non-functional. In a span from almost immediate transformation to a period of about three days, but usually in one or two days, the skin slits along the back and the spinner (imago) emerges. The body color is more vibrant now, and the wings are often transparent or hyaline; tails are long and delicate, and the forelegs of the male become quite long. This second-winged stage is unique to the mayflies. Sexually mature now, many mating flights occur when air temperatures are in the sixty to seventy degree range. In the typical mating flight, the males appear over the water, rising and falling as a swarm. The females fly into the undulating swarm to secure mates. Mating occurs in flight and the female deposits the eggs to the water. Some are jettisoned above the surface, some species dip periodically to the surface, some lie prone to the surface, and the species of

The mayfly spinner typically has a vibrantly colored body and transparent (hyaline) wings. The tails are lengthened. In the case of the males, the forelegs become quite long.

As mayfly nymphs approach the time of transformation to winged adults, the wing pads typically darken and become almost black in some species.

At the time of the actual transformation, the thorax area splits and the adult mayfly dun struggles free of the restraining nymphal shuck.

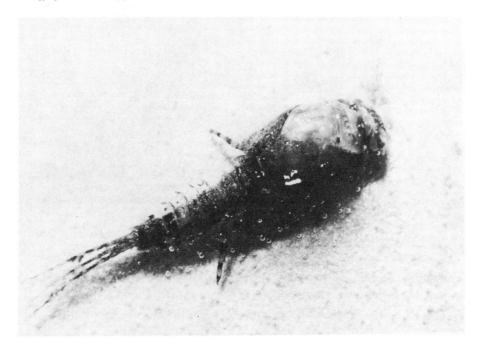

Baetis crawl beneath the water surface to deposit their eggs.

The females then lie spent on the surface as do many males. However, some males survive another day or a few days before succumbing.

STONEFLIES: As you might imagine, the name is an implication of their preference for well-aerated, rocky, stream sections and in some cases, the wave-lapped, highly-oxygenated shallows of large lakes.

In a manner similar to the mayfly they have an incomplete metamorphis or life cycle consisting of egg, nymph, and adult. Depending on the species (some 400 occur in North America), the nymphs vary in size with average body lengths ranging from less than half an inch to about two inches. Underwater life spans range from a year to about three years. Colors vary with species. Some are almost uniform in coloration: cream, green, pale amber to brownish black and grayish black. Others exhibit a paling or lightening on their undersides and a few are quite striking in contrasting blacks and yellows. Their nymphal feeding habits are different according to the species, and the other includes vegetarians and carnivorous forms.

The stoneflies moult several times as they grow. When fully grown they migrate to favored rocks or to the shallows and climb out of the water. The thorax is split and the adult struggles free. Adults often rest for some time while the soft wings and body parts harden. Many emerge at night or very early in the day; occasionally some emerge during the day. Because emergences are often so slow, their favored nighttime and early day emergences are

The stonefly nymphs are typically flattened in appearance, feature "double" wing pads, and prefer well-aerated stream sections.

---

probably an adaptation to prevent predatory birds from truly devastating their ranks. Western anglers eagerly await the so-called salmon fly or willow fly hatches on large swift streams. These streams are ideally suited to the habits of the stonefly. Huge trout are willing to feed on these emergences.

Adult stoneflies are clumsy fliers. They almost appear to be walking or running through the air as they fly with their bodies held in an almost vertical position. The females of many species discharge the egg mass by dipping the

The stone nymphs climb out of the water prior to transformation to the adult stage. The thorax and head area split and the emerging adult struggles free in a time-consuming process.

The stonefly adult features an elongated body. Its wings fold flat over the body when it is at rest.

tip of the abdomen below the surface while in flight. This can trigger explosive rises from opportunistic trout. Except for mating flights, stoneflies are rarely over the water in great numbers. Still, there is a prolonged availability of one species or another throughout the season. Patterns tied to suggest the available stoneflies always offer potential success in appropriate waters.

Caddis are another insect of great importance to the angler. They have a complete metamorphosis consisting of egg, larva, pupa, and adult. Various species have adopted to life in virtually all water types. Some 800 species occur in North America. They are variable in length as larva, from the so-called micro caddis of one-eighth of an inch to lengths of some two inches. The larval forms are most interesting as many of them build protective cases about themselves, the cases cemented together by glandular secretions. Despite a possible rough exterior to the cases, the insides are quite smooth, allowing a freedom of movement. There are characteristic patterns within various species. Typical materials utilized are leaf fragments, sticks, bits of barks or twigs or other vegetation, sand grains, tiny stones, and even tiny shells. There is a seeming precision and uniformity. Most species repeatedly make the same type of case from the same materials.

As larva grows it adds to the cases. Often the larva lies with the head, thorax and legs outside the case and the body is mildly undulated to keep water circulating. Although some of the cases appear heavy and awkward, they are usually built by those living in fast waters where the weight is of anchoring value. Further, a bubble or two of air inside can provide buoyancy and make it relatively weightless. Some species do not build cases through the first few instars. Some remain free living throughout their larval life span. These build a silken net or tube so fastened to stones that the current washes through it. The larva lying in a silken or stonewalled retreat nearby can feed on the trapped food forms. Some construct partial cases, faced with the silken nets behind which the larval forms remain to feed on tiny organisms trapped in the netting. All these larva forms are of value to trout food and many imitations exist. Most imitations suggest the round-bodied, wormlike larva alone; some few attempt to suggest the cased larva, for trout consume larva and case when given the opportunity. They eventually pass the bits of bark and twigs or whatever, while their digestive processes utilize the larva.

The pupal stage follows the larval stage. Often this is a ten-day and two-week period. Adult characteristics begin to appear as the transformation takes place. The retreat makers construct an elliptical cocoon in which they pupate. Case makers pupate within their own case. They may cement the case down. It may have a silken screen spun across the opening, or a protective pebble may block the opening. The pupa typically remain active within the case, undulating the body to provide water motion.

When the proper elapsed time has been achieved, the pupa cuts out of the restraining case and swims or struggles to the surface. At the surface the pupal husk ruptures and the adult emerges. Some caddis complete this change on the bottom and swim to the surface and out of the water. Some slow-water species crawl to the shallows and emerge like stone flies.

Caddis emergences are productive times for the angler. Trout must actively chase moving species. Tell-tale rolling and splashing may indicate activity. Surface disturbances are possible during pupal activity as the trout roll and slash near the surface. Unless the surface rise form is accompanied by a bubble

Many caddis larvae inhabit protective cases that are striking and distinctive by species. At left is a larva form in a case of vegetative fragments. At right a stone or pebble protective case. At front right is a caddis larva that has been removed from its case.

The caddis fly adult has a distinctive "tent wing" appearance making it easily distinguishable from the flat wing stoneflies or the upright wing mayfly forms.

or bubbles, the pupal suggestions are apt to be most appropriate. Adult caddis are obviously fine fare for the trout as well. During egg laying activity there may be fine trout activity. Some species oviposit over the water, some dip the eggs into the stream itself, some species go beneath the surface to oviposit directly on the bottom. All activities lend themselves to succesful imitation. Various caddis may be expected to be available on a season long basis.

The midges of the order *Diptera* encompass every aquatic community. Yet

31

the greatest angling potential may well lie in lush, weedy areas, slower stream sections, and ponds and lakes. The high altitude ponds at or above timberline are other general locations where midge imitations may be essential to success. Many larger aquatic forms are not universally represented in the high country, yet some midge forms are almost always available and assume a very significant importance in spite of their relative size.

There is a complete metamorphosis of egg, larva, pupa and adult. The latter three stages are worthy of imitation. Despite their relative size, typically one-eighth to half an inch, the virtual season-long availability of the differing forms plus their vast numerical abundance and relative ease of capture requires imitations at one time or another.

The round-bodied larva come in different colors. Commonly they are red, yellowish, almost translucent white, greenish, grey or brownish black. For practical reasons involving their small size and ease of strike detection, the larva imitations are best presented gently to visibly feeding fish. It is possible to fish them deeply with slow retrieves, but on the whole you'll be more concerned with near surface activity.

Many species spend the day deep and rise toward the surface with approaching evening. In those magic twilight moments the trout may be apparently rising but not moving to your tiny dries. They may pluck at leader knots and you'll see them roll and flash. Even backs or tails will disturb the surface. Most likely larval or pupal imitations are required when the dries drift unmolested by the abundant and active trout. After the larva transforms to the pupal stage, there is ample evidence of the ultimate adult. Differing from the roundish, wormlike larva, the pupa shows definite hairy appendages at the head and tail, folded (but visible on close inspection) wings, as well as obvious thorax enlargement. These drifting pupa are taken avidly. During the transformation from pupa to adult there is trout activity. The transformation is time consuming and they are exteemely vulnerable. Adults typically are mosquitolike in appearance and may sit quietly on the water for some time before taking flight. Again, a period of vulnerability.

Start with tiny dries during this action. If they aren't effective, the pupal or larval imitations should be tried. Get a sample of the insect to determine developmental stage, form, and color. This is usually possible. There may also be a hint available in inspection of the rise-form type. If you've ever tried to pick an insect from water by letting it wash into your hand, you've found it impossible. The surface tension diverts the insect around your hand. The trout has a similar problem, but also has a built-in solution. He flares his gills, and the insect, air, and water are taken in. Then the air is expelled through the gills, leaving a bubble or bubbles in the wake of the rise form. If bubbles exist in the rise form, it is likely the insect was taken in or on the surface. An appropriate imitation may be used. Without the bubble evidence, more than likely a pupa or larva imitation should be fished just beneath the surface. This bubble evidence has other applications. Was the trout slashing to the caddis pupa barely beneath the surface or to the emerged adult, the barely subsurface mayfly nymph or the adult? Such clues or signals sometimes help us sort out the probabilities, guiding us to appropriate fly type selection.

Another relative deserves at least passing mention: the crane fly. The larva are wormlike, typically from half an inch to about two inches, with colorations varying from a whitish shading through pale orange tones to various brownish shadings. The larva will often be grubbed off the bottom. Imitiations fished on a deep, dead, drift can be effective. Most (not all) pupate out of water and are not important to the angler. Adults may be suggested by various, high-riding, sparse types, such as spiders, skaters, and variants, although there are a few specific patterns tied for a more precise imitation of the adult's gangly, spraddle-legged posture.

Let's glance at a few other important insects. From the insect order *Odonata* there are dragon flies and damselflies. Generally the nymphal imitations are more successful than the adult imitations, although some effective adult imitations do exist. Nymphal forms of these two insects are visibly distinguishable. The damselflies are slender and minnowlike with a body terminating in three flat gills. Dragonflies are husky, almost muscular in appearance. Although modes of locomotion differ, both are capable of active movement. They are predatory forms ranging about the bottom amidst the weed beds, searching for their food forms. Sunken suggestions fished in a stuttering pause and pull motion can be very effective. Towards emergence time they crawl from the water and ascend reeds and plant stems. Their empty husks may be seen in a manner similar to the stone flies, and their discarded nymphal shucks can be found on stream rocks. Emergence takes place early in the day and is also time consuming. The adults are at first soft bodied with a shriveled abdomen and crumpled wings. Before they can take off, they must extend their abdomen and expand and dry their wings. Once more, this early emergence probably takes place to avoid predatory birds which would be active at later hours. Nymphal colors are usually in the olive to greenish brown values. At times windy days and egg laying activities provide good activity for the adult suggestions, but the nymph patterns generally do better.

The hellgrammite and the allied alderflies and fishflies may be of seasonal or local importance. The hellgrammite is a highly regarded bass bait which is also effective on large trout. It is the larva of the huge dobsonfly. As larva they are secretive and have a long, three-year life cycle. Consequently they are available to fish in a range of sizes up to three inch monsters. Imitations of one and one quarter inch to two inches are most productive. They handle well and move fish nicely. The larva have a flattened, busy-looking appearance with tufted gills along the sides. The brownish black imitations should be fished in the swift sections where the natural larvae are abundant.

The alderflies have a basic larval shape similar to the hellgrammite but are considerably smaller: about one inch or a bit less. The larva are brownish and thick skinned with a single-fringed tail gill. Adults are caddislike in appearance and are often active in bright spring sunlight. The aquatic habitat includes ponds, lakes and streams. The alderfly pattern is an effective imitiation of the smokey to dark-winged flies.

In the fishfly there is again a superficial resemblance to the larger hellgrammite, yet the fringed gills are lacking, The fishfly lateral gills are slender. Also, there are no strong mandibles as on the hellgrammite. Fishflies are more widely distributed in various water types. A typical larval imitation of about one inch is effective in dark brownish to brownish black values.

The small crustacea that assume significant value in weedy streams and ponds are the scuds and sow bugs. Often they are called freshwater shrimp by anglers. The scuds are from the order *Amphipoda*. You may also hear them referred to as side swimmers. Shrimplike in appearance, they are flattened sideways or laterally compressed. These omnivorous scavengers feed on plant and animal debris. In turn they are consumed by trout in large numbers. They lie close to the bottom or among submerged weed growths in ponds and slow-flowing streams, and are especially abundant in rich alkaline waters. The sizes vary from $3/8$ to almost an inch. The colors are typically grayish, yellowish gray, tan to light brown, and olive. They move on their sides by flexing and extending their entire body and frequently rolling on their sides or back. The bodies are held out straight while swimming.

The sow bugs are from the order *Isopoda* and are often abundant in rich, alkaline waters amidst watercress and weed where they are omnivorous scavengers. They are seldom in open water. Most species prefer shallow waters. Average sizes may be from about a quarter of an inch to a bit over half an inch. Most are uniformly gray, or almost black. A few are brownish, reddish, or yellowish. They have a flattened appearance and feature fourteen legs. Imitations of these dead bugs drifted by the weed bed edges are effective.

Crayfish are from the order *Decapoda*. They too may be quite appealing to large trout, although not too many imitations are generally available. Although they can reach large sizes, your imitations are best in the smaller sizes for reasons of reasonable suggestion, handling ease, and a fish preference for the smaller, more manageable sizes. Imitations can be moved over those rocky runs where the naturals preside. Very early in the day and very late, even into darkness, are apt to be the most productive times. Many of the larger trout in late spring have eaten crayfish. These are a vastly overlooked possibility for big trout.

The bugs of aquatic representation are from the order *Hemiptera*. The water boatman or corixa bug are common to shallow waters of ponds, lakes and streams. Many species are dark grayish and often mottled with dark brownish black and may be faintly cross lined with yellow. Their long hind legs are flattened for swimming and extend out, like the backswimmers, and can propel the bug along with strong oarlike strokes. They are very buoyant. When submerged they must hold onto plants or weeds or other objects to remain submerged. They dive with great ease and agility, and air taken in at the surface usually surrounds them in a silvery envelope. A typical imitation may be about a quarter inch in overall body length.

The backswimmers have a boat-shaped or keeled back and paddlelike legs.

The hind legs are longer than the middle and front legs. They hold an air supply on the underside of their bodies and beneath the wings, and come to the surface periodically to rest and replenish their air supply by sticking the tip of their abdomens above the surface. They can and will bite sharply. When diving or beneath the surface they exhibit a silvery envelope of air bubbles and are capable of moving with excellent agility. Of the various species, the most common is about half an inch long with a dark brownish olive body and light and dark mottling of the wing cases.

The leeches of the class *Hirudinea* are another, occasionally important, food form. They are usually dorsoventrally flattened, sometimes brightly colored, and patterned in green and black. Some species swim well, others swim poorly. In the last few years commercial "snakelike" patterns have become available and have proven quite effective on large trout.

The land dwelling terrestrial insects are not aquatic but leap, tumble, or are blown to the water with some regularity and become important food forms. The more important imitative problems usually center around grasshoppers, crickets, beetles, leafhoppers, inchworms and ants (both winged and without wings). Each of these forms exhibit a distinctive shape or silhouette that can be suggested by widely available commercial patterns.

The baitfish constitute another realm of opportunity and imitative potential. There are various shiners, chubs, darters, dace, sculpin and others, including imitations of small trout that can work well. These serve as prototypes for a host of streamer-bucktail patterns. Have some of those forms available in the waters you fish, and back this up with a couple of bright, attractor patterns for those times when the water is off color or when you've run out of better ideas.

Lefty Kreh fishing on the Savage River in western Maryland's mountains.

4.

READING WATER

Streams

Learning to read water is an acquired skill. Experience is the best teacher. Admittedly this takes time, but the novice may be able to hasten the process by enlisting the aid of an experienced angler. Invariably such experienced hands are more than willing to assist and explain why trout station themselves at definite stream locations. In your own early angling experiences think about why the trout rising are rising where they are, what combination of currents and nearby cover exists, where the emerging insects are drifting, and what are the feeding lies of the trout. All these bits and pieces of information eventually sort themselves out and an instinct for rapid and accurate appraisal develops.

To assist in this learning process we can cover some of the fundamental considerations affecting their location. The primary need of the trout is security: protection or concealment from potential predators. They also seek protection from very strong mainstream currents which would rapidly tire them. They do, however, like to have a current flow nearby for food forms on the assorted drift which the current brings. Another obvious requirement is suitable water temperature. In critically warm situations they seek out spring holes, cold water seepages, and areas of the stream with increased oxygen contents or cooler temperatures. For our introductory purposes we can assume water temperatures to be suitable and simply examine some typical situations.

Trout are both territorial and dominant. Invariably the better fish select and maintain the best feeding and sheltering lies. We should also note that water velocity is not constant from top to bottom. This becomes apparent when standing in a waist deep flow of water. The surface flow tugs at our waist, at our upper thighs we feel a faster current force being exerted, while at our booted feet a much reduced velocity is noticed. The current similarly slows near large obstructions and along stream banks, for friction causes a lateral slow-down. The water close to the bank runs slower than the main current just a short distance away.

These considerations have important bearings on trout locations. For instance, in moderately deep runs the fish show an unequal distribution from top to bottom. Beneath the strong current of the main run the bottom is apt to be rocks, boulders, and gravel. There is already a quiet cushion of water close to the bottom and the presence of such rocks further deflects and cushions the flow. The depth of water is ideal concealment and provides the diffusion of light or shade which is more comfortable to the lidless eye of the trout. Many bottom-dwelling food forms exist here, and other stream-drifted insects and food forms which are washed deep may be easily snapped up. These deep runs deserve investigative probings with your flies or lures. If an emergence of insects is taking place, the trout may be holding high, a few inches from the surface, with their attention on the drifting flies. If the main current is too forceful for a comfortable position maintenance, they move to the side of the main currents or drop back in the run to a point where velocities are reduced and they may hold with relative ease.

The undercut banks are excellent locations. There is overhead cover and a cushioning zone of quiet water with easy access to a primary, food-supplying current.

Although some food develops in virtually all water types, the stream riffle areas are most important in this respect. If they are very shallow the fish may only move in when foraging actively or during an emergence of insects. The diminished light values of predawn and evening may bring foraging fish into these areas. If, by chance, the riffle is a couple of feet deep, it could be considered a trout holding possibility at any time and fished through thorough-ly.

The riffles typically shelve or drop into a pool. Toward the head of the pool is the deeper water. With any kind of appropriate bottom structure, trout may be expected to hold here in comfort. These fish have first opportunity at food drifting into the pool. When a hatch is in progress they simply move up towards the surface to feed. If the main current tongue is too swift, they again migrate to the current edges or drop back in the pool to a point where the current force is diminished and they can comfortably hold and feed. It's also possible that some fish will move directly up into the riffle area ahead of the pool. At the tail of the pool the water shallows and may, if cover is available, provide another fine lie. Many times appropriate tail cover is lacking and fish move back into these tailing shallows only when in a definite feeding posture.

The long flat stretches of shallow, slow-moving water can be very deceptive. They deserve a look before you pass premature judgment and hurry on. There is a particular stretch of a nearby river that is overlooked on one side by a high bank. From it the stretch appears absolutely barren. Mainstream bottom cover is virtually nonexistent and every pebble and grain of sand seems visible. Yet every summer evening there are quiet rise forms here and there, especially close to the opposite shore. Wading over and walking slowly along that far bank reveals a few of the secrets. There is an occasional deeper depression in the stream bed, perhaps scoured by a current deflection in the high water of spring. There are occasional hollowed out root structures among the streamside willows. Another depression exists in the stream bottom behind the fallen tree. Each, by itself, seems insignificant, but they total up to a dozen or more individual lies that contain a trout or two. It's tough water to "just fish," but during any emergence activity the trout become vulnerable to careful stalking and deliberate presentations. Easily overlooked, this is proof that trout can seemingly disappear into the strangest places.

The pocket water stretches are quickly flowing currents, diverted and broken by boulders and large rocks. The obstructions provide any number of quiet water cushions and hiding places. Pocket water also harbors excellent insect populations. During periods of warm water there are increased oxygen levels here as compared to other water types. This is an obvious attraction for the comfort-seeking trout. Waterfall pools may also prove productive, especially when the pool bottom is broken and diverse with rocks or sunken logs.

Some streams have a steep gradient, which puts a premium on short, quick and accurate casting. Many anglers bypass the bubbly waters formed as the currents flow smooth and slick over the rocks and drop down into what might be called miniature waterfalls. But that bubbly water is often productive. The water flow energy is actually dissipated for a brief moment before it gathers and flows on. Insects washed into these areas may be submerged and swirled about helplessly before being pushed on downstream. I've often found trout willing to take large nymphs or wets plopped into these areas when other water types were non-productive.

Some stream banks also provide hiding and feeding areas, and not all of these are obvious. Some are insignificant in initial appearance. There is a good example nearby in the midst of a heavily fished section of stream. Few bother with this particular site. Standing below it and looking upstream we see the left bank shelving very gradually off into the stream, providing no semblance of cover or concealment. The right hand bank is low and inconspicuous but it is tree lined and the small current that comes through here is diverted toward that right side bank. The browns that take up residence here find shelter in washed out root structures along that right hand bank. During emergence activity they move out mere inches. This is a consistent producer to those in the know. Activity is always quiet, always tight by the bank, and the average angler wanders by with a cursory glance that fails to reveal the real value of this run. Similar situations exist on all trout waters.

Meadow stream banks offer a modified, but essentially parallel situation with their numerous undercuts and overhanging grasses. The bank-feeding fish with their quiet, unhurried rise forms are often the largest fish that surface-feed on these streams. On spring creeks and those weedy multi-channeled streams, the bank edges must also be watched carefully. Also there are excellent insect and crustacean populations in the abundant watercress and islands of *elodea* of these stream types. These weeds form obstructions that divert the flow and

Western meadow streams may provide exceptional angling. Watch the stream banks for quiet rise forms which may mask large trout.

With numerous rocks and obstructions to deflect main current flows and provide cushions of quiet water for the trout, this section of a western river offers excellent angling potential.

create channels in the same manner that fallen trees and rocks might do on another water type. These channels should be probed by the thorough angler.

By reading a stream you're trying to locate those areas where security for the trout is available with a potential feeding area nearby: those areas where fast and slow waters merge; those slow-water "islands" in the midst of faster flows; sunken logs lying parallel to the current flow; eddying currents supporting trapped insect forms; currents rejoining below islands that have split and diverted the main flow; edges where shallow water falls abruptly off to deeper areas; above, below and beside large in-stream rocks and other singular obstructions. These and more are all typical. As we've said previously, when you see activity, try to analyze why it is taking place and where it is taking place. Trout activity is not random. The more bits and pieces of information you file away, the quicker and more accurate your future stream reading appraisals will be.

Ponds and Lakes

Ponds and lakes are inherently more difficult to analyze. The moving water of a stream always provides clues that eventually become familiar and meaningful. The lake surface is simply there, almost defying you to probe for its secrets. Just as there are various stream types, there are different lake and pond types. A backwoods pond at 2500 feet in the Adirondacks is a different situation than a pond tucked away at 10,000 feet on a Colorado mountain. Still, there are possibilities in each, not the least of which is fine angling for large fish.

Cherished by many is the discovery of a newly formed beaver pond. Intimate and newly enriched, rapid trout growth occurs. Eventually the waters become much too acidic and warm, causing the trout population to rapidly decline. But, these ponds at their prime offer excellent potential. Their dark waters are best probed with wet flies, nymphs, or midget streamers, unless definite surface activity is taking place. Wading the small beaver ponds with their soft muck and debris is distrubing, difficult, and potentially dangerous. Crouching and creeping along the stick jam platform is usually possible. The old mainstream channel is apt to be productive when the fish are down during bright sunlight days. Any cruising activity near shore or around still, standing trees will be self-evident when it occurs. A small inflatable boat or float tube may be advantageous on some waters.

In New England the beaver pond specialists are very secretive, realizing that such waters have a short productive cycle. One individual, in addition to his own locating efforts, is continually probing the local trappers, hunters, hikers, anglers, and wardens to learn of new sites from year to year. Any possibilities are carefully marked on a topo map for further investigation.

Another overlooked resource is by any swampy area that is either the headwater area of a stream or a portion of the lake itself. A small inflatable boat or float tube is often required, but these areas are sometimes deep, clear, spring fed and almost undisturbed.

In general the food generating areas of lakes are shallow, to the depths of sunlight penetration. Deep waters located near such shallows provide an escape route for wary trout. Whenever there are shallows which suddenly fall away to the depths, they are potentially excellent feeding sites, especially early and late in the day. Out on the lake proper near any island there is often a bouldery bottom for a short distance until another abrupt drop-off occurs. Shoals or reefs that swell up close to the surface are also potential feeding areas.

Spring hole locations are excellent during periods of hot weather and are apt to draw concentrations of trout seeking relief from the excessively warm surrounding waters. Tom Sobolewski, who operates Clark's Tackle in Lake Placid, advised Tony Atwill and I that he often swims his favorite Adirondack ponds to find these spring hole locations. Several hot hours later as Tony and I backpacked into a reasonably offbeat area of the western Adirondacks, the words of Tom Sobolewski seemed to make a lot of sense. However, when we stood at the shoreline of our destination and noticed several leeches, apparently just waiting for us, we decided to abandon any swimming in favor of our inflatable boats. Several times spring holes will be marked by a single "push pole." Someone has previously pinpointed the location and marked it by shoving a long branch into the bottom. When these seem to appear at random in odd locations they are worth checking out on remote waters. *New York Times* outdoor columnist Nelson Bryant is an experienced outdoorsman with a special affinity for remote ponds. He thoroughly believes in deeply sunken flies worked around spring hole locations during midsummer heat on his favored northeastern ponds. On a day hike into the Green Mountain National Forest area, Nelson was actively moving about the pond in his inflatable boat, trying to locate those elusive drop-offs and spring holes. Using a rock as an anchor and a probe he began searching according to a theory he attributed to Thoreau: "... the deepest part of the pond is often where imaginary lines, connecting its longest and widest parts, intersect."

Additionally, the inlets and outlets of lakes are always worth investigation as well as any thoroughfares between a series of ponds or lakes.

In weedy waters the channels between the emergent growth should be probed thoroughly. These waters are rich in insect and crustacean life forms and are often superb for large trout. On weedy waters the dragonfly and damselfly nymphs often move toward emergent weed growths early in the predawn. Husky trout follow suit. Sunken imitations, fished in a stuttering pause and pull manner may be productive. It is certainly a good idea to watch the surface in the evening. Just as on the streams, the pond-dwelling trout often forage actively early and late in the day. At times help may be available in the form of a distinctive shoreline. For example, a gradually sloping shoreline usually continues to fall away underwater. A steep shoreline falling sharply to the lake probably continues the same way underwater. There may be several

Float tubes or belly boats can be a valuable addition for the angler/backpacker, permitting water coverage that would otherwise be impossible.

feet of water close to shore with a bouldery, rock strewn bottom that offers food and cover. Check to see if there is any regional or local fishing literature showing pond or stream drop-offs.

Lake fish also cruise for food. If they are rising, the experienced angler will watch the direction of the rises and then lead the fish by casting well ahead of their travel direction. Watch too, for feeding lanes on breezy days when the surface drift is being blown toward windward shores. Sometimes there will be slicks of calmer water with trout cruising the area for trapped insect forms.

If the winds come up strong they may cause a good feeding period along the windward shore. Early in the windy period the best activity is at or near the surface. If the winds continue, fish tend to switch and work deeper as the continuing wave action ultimately sets up a return current flow deep beneath the surface influence.

The ponds that lie at high altitudes are a variation of the overall problem. There is apt to be a less diverse aquatic community. Generally the most important high country food forms are scuds, midges, mayflies, caddis flies, and terrestrials, although their relative importance varies from one body of water to another. Sometimes there is one or two minnow species available even though the so-called trash fish are virtually non-existent at these altitudes. These high country waters may be the ultimate for the backpacking angler, lying in regions of majestic beauty and solitude. The weather is variable to say the least, the seasons are short, and winterkill of fish may be a problem in some shallow waters. But, if you are at the right place at the right time, there is nothing quite like it. High country specialists utilize inlets and outlets the same way that we would check these areas at lower altitudes. Look for various natural drainage areas as well. These are sites where snow melt, springs, or rain runoffs have gone into the pond. Fish sometimes gather at these sites despite the original water source possibly having dried up. Very early and late in the day, the best location is often a shelf that may extend out into the lake for a short distance, then abruptly drops off to much deeper water. If you have a float tube or inflatable boat along, cast from the deep open water back towards this shelf, working the fly in the direction of the deep water. If there is no tube or boat, try casts made parallel to this shelf (unless there is specific, visible activity to zero in on).

Any points of land that extend into the pond are also worth looking into. Cruising trout have to go around these points and may come within easy reach of the bank-bound angler.

Ponds and lakes may be considerably different than the flowing waters of the streams but, in time, they too will reveal their secrets to your advantage.

5.

INTRODUCTION TO METHODS

The freedom of travel associated with backpacking permits access to a variety of water types and sizes. Thus an overview of a typical stream course should help the novice angler anticipate angling requirements. Most streams are zonally divisible. Their characteristics change greatly from the headwater areas to the ultimate destination where the stream joins a larger river system, lake, or ocean. Some of the differences are physical size, width, depth, flow volume, water types, gradient, and temperature ranges. These differences have some bearing on typical angling approaches, the food forms available to the trout, and the species of trout in numerical dominance.

In hilly or mountainous country the upper reaches are usually small, intimate, well aerated, often tree canopied and shady with cooler average temperatures being maintained through the midsummer heat. Because of the intimate nature of the small stream, there is a close association with shore life in that some terrestrials such as ants, beetles, and crickets fall or tumble to the water regularly to supplement the aquatic insect availability. Those streams with headwaters in meadowy areas also contribute quantities of grasshoppers seasonally. The intimate, generally shallower waters imply easier animal and diving bird predator access. The dominant trout populations tend to be those which do best in non-competetive situations or those with a preference for cooler average water temperatures (i.e. western cutthroat and eastern brook trout). Available aquatic insect forms are less varied and less abundant than in lower stream sections. The midges, cased and net spinning caddis, small mayfly nymphs, some stoneflies in the quicker runs, and perhaps a minnow species or two usually are the dominant food forms.

If there are occasional deeper holes, runs or undercuts, these tend to be the prime locations for the occasional mini-stream native trophy. There may be seasonal headwater penetration or migration from other species as spring-spawning rainbows or fall-spawning browns move up. Also, if lower stream stretches become unsuitably warm in midsummer dry spells, there may be some migration of larger mainstream fish working up these cooler tributaries and headwater areas. In the event there is adequate cover and food, a few of these larger fish may take up permanent residence. The vast majority simply drop back down to the larger water areas as it becomes appropriate to do so. Still, I've seen many an outsize trout in streams that could be jumped across in many places.

A fine Cutthroat from a small spring creek near Jackson Hole, Wyoming.

These intimate little waters have an intrigue all their own. Pleasant and productive, they are the stream types most commonly associated with back-pack angling. There is less stream pressure, summer temperatures are cooler, and the trout are less selective as natural food availability is more restricted. Certainly most of the trout run to the small sizes, but there are those occasional large fish bonuses. Besides, the backpacking angler's equipment needs are minimal. Usually wading is neither required nor is it recommended. A careful shorebound approach supplemented by occasional judicious rock hopping or just plain wet wading will do the trick. Exercise care in stream approaches, utilizing natural cover whenever possible and keep clothing on the drab, inconspicuous side. Work progressively but fairly rapidly for best results. The light-weight spin fisherman will find tiny spinners productive with lightweight plugs, jigs and spoons also appropriate for the occasional deep holes, runs, or dark undercuts. The fly rodder can get by with just a floating line in most such waters. If flies need to be worked deep, the addition of a split shot or twist-on lead about eighteen inches above the fly is usually adequate. The available food forms imply that small dries, wets, nymphs, a couple of terrestrials, and a midget streamer or bucktail are appropriate.

Brushy, snaggy streams are common in many areas and can provide excellent fishing. Here, Dick Pobst works close to the cover.

By midsummer on those mountain streams with a steep gradient, some of the better fish lurk by and beneath the bubbly areas formed as the water flows over the rocks and drops into the heads of pools. Since trout are opportunistic, large high floating patterns are surprisingly effective. These big dries are durable, visible, and tempting. Some of the types well suited to this prospecting are the Wulff patterns, the Humpy, the Irresistible, and any of the Bivisibles. Try #10's, even on small streams. If a large fish swirls and misses, reference the spot for a bit later. Chances are he'll move to the fly again. This is usually upstream work, except when unusual stream configurations call for approaching from above and drifting a fly down into the best cover.

Further downstream the gradient lessens and the stream begins to broaden. These midreaches are generally the peak trout fishing sections of the entire stream. Water types may be diverse with larger pools, runs, riffles, and pocket water alternately available. Temperatures are more moderate than in the headwater areas and the aquatic communities show much greater diversification as appropriate habitat and food is available to them in greater abundance.

The conventional stream-bred insects as well as various crustaceans and an expanded baitfish community may all be on hand and require simulation. Typically, browns and rainbows dominate these middle reaches. Angling methods are more diverse and there are periods of selective feeding. In the heat of summer the most appropriate times to fish are early and late in the day unless specific insect activity is taking place which tempts the trout to active feeding.

The lower stream sections often become marginal trout waters as streams flatten out, coursing the valley floor. They are typically wider, deeper, much warmer, and offer less diversity of water type. As temperatures become more suitable to other species such as bass, pike, panfish, etc., these fish begin to dominate. Trout are few, but often very large. Big browns seem especially adept at locating the right combination of depth, cover, or cooling temperature influence from spring seepages or incoming tributaries. They wax fat on the abundance of forage fish and other food forms. Fishing is slow and, to an extent, specialized. Generally dry fly moments are rare, but the prospecting and persistent angler adept at handling deeply sunken nymphs, wets, and streamers may hook a real trophy brown.

Thus, the course of a single stream will ultimately demand a variety of techniques and methods. The beginning angler is advised to maintain an open mind toward these requirements and utilize whatever method is suitable to the water and the activity. Many fly fishermen develop a strong preference for a particular method and use it to the exclusing of more appropriate methods. Obviously any individual preference is defensible from a standpoint of enjoyment, but it also limits fish-taking potential. I feel that this limits the total enjoyment available from the sport. Each method (dry, wet, nymph, terrestrial or streamer) has much to offer. Each is complex enough so that complete books can, have been, and will continue to be written about the subtle nuances of each. The novice angler is advised to follow up our introductory theme by studying more complete references.

The wet fly is a versatile approach which has been neglected in recent years as increased emphasis has been placed on nymph pattern and method development. The wet approach is usually considered to be broadly suggestive of aquatic activity, whereas the nymph implies greater specificity of imitation. Frequently the distinctions are blurred and there is some obvious overlapping of the two methods. Normally trout are specific and selective in their feeding when there is an adequate availability of a food form to warrant such exclusivity; the remainder of the time their activity is non-specific and opportunistic. Therefore, the impressionistic wet fly is frequently a sound starting point with which to search the water. Since it is suggestively lifelike there is a great deal of latitude hidden in the method: casts can be angled toward any compass point; the stream can be worked in up or down directions; the flies may dead drift or be animated variously; the working of all different water levels from the surface film down through middepths and gravel scratching levels is possible. The use of more than one fly on a single leader offers possible variations in the drifting depths of the flies as well as contrast in pattern, size, and tonal value.

Searching the water should be done in a thoroughly progressive manner with casting cycles hitting nearby water first then gradually radiating out to cover medium distances and finally the longer fishing arcs.

On a seasonal basis, the early mayflies tend to do quite a bit of drifting and spasmodic struggling to escape the nymphal shuck. The cast directed somewhat up and across stream and then permitted to alternately dead drift and twitch gently is often effective.

Another staple approach is the natural or dead drift. Of the various ways to achieve this, one of the best is to direct the cast well upstream and across with enough slack to permit the start of a free drift. As the slack is taken up by the current the line is mended to compensate and restore the free drifting motion of the artifical. Mending is simply throwing a loop of line up or downstream, whichever will permit the continuation of the drift. As the fly passes across stream from you and continues downstream, it is continually mended as required. This creates the illusion of the detached helpless insect form at the mercy of the current, assures a drift in harmony with existing current flows, and the fly is apt to remain sideways to that flow (the most visible position to the upstream facing trout). Across and downstream from you the fly will begin to elevate and move slightly towards your side of the stream on the tightening line. Many strikes occur here as the illusion is that of an insect suddenly coming to life and heading for the surface and airborne safety. If no strikes occur, the line continues to swing, coming to rest directly downstream from your position. It should not be immediately retrieved as it can become subject to various possibilities. Hold it steady, animate it by slowly raising and lowering the rod, raise the rod slowly towards the vertical and then lower it and shake out additional slack. Or, if there is deep cover along your side, lower the rod tip to the stream bed and retrieve the fly deep and close to the open side of the cover. Browns especially like overhead cover and a fly must work very deep to be seen.

At times a cross-stream swim is excellent. Take a position opposite or a bit above the suspected lie of the fish and drop the fly a few feet upstream and a bit beyond the lie of the fish. When the fly touches the surface allow it to dead drift across the hoped for taking lie or, more commonly, elevate the rod to keep as much line as possible off the water and flutter the fly back across the stream. This is especially telling in a two-fly set up with the twitching flies activiated by rod tip or line-hand manipulations. The two-fly approach is also good on cross and downstream presentations. About the easiest method of rigging up is to simply extend the heavier material end used when connecting leader sections in a barrel knot.

Another quick way to add a dropper to a knotted leader is to take a short section of separate monofilament and form a loop in one end. Then, loop it around the main body of the leader above a leader knot. It will hold in place against the leader knot. Keep the dropper strands on the short side, say four to six inches. If flies of different sizes are being used in a two-fly setup the larger of the two normally goes on the end of the leader and the smaller one on the dropper strand. The starting point is contrast in size, pattern, and color. Broken pocket water usually fishes well to the two-fly approach. Work a short line and allow the flies to drift and drag naturally in and out of quiet waters below and beside the stream obstructions. When natural drifts fail to produce, work cross-stream casts with the rod elevated and strip the flies. The dropper should alternately skim the surface, become elevated and drag below the surface.

Another appropriate time for a pair of wets is after a midsummer rain with the stream rising and becoming discolored. Nymphs and streamers also produce well at this time, but the down and across approach of a pair of wets usually works.

On small streams, and when fish are working near the top on larger waters, the floating line is adequate. For greater depths the sinktip or true sinking line may be more appropriate.

The basic nymphing methods encompass all the standard wet fly approaches and add a few singular opportunities. A very effective fast-water, short-line deeply sunken method involves a well-greased floating line (and it's usually preferable to grease the upper two feet or so of the leader butt), twist-on leads and a weighted nymph. The leader should be long, about twelve or more feet. Although various casting angles are possible, the usual approach is upstream and somewhat across. After the cast is made, the line is brought to the rod-

Mending line is required to restore or maintain a natural drift in all fly rodding methods. With the rod in front, roll or flip the rod up or down stream, whichever is required. Mending corrections vary from short and subtle tip motions to vigorous full arm mends depending on conditions.

holding hand. All retrieves are done behind this hand. As this is a dead drift method, there should be no line drag. Usually it is best to strip the line and let it drop rather than to try coiling it in the line hand. Any belly formed by varying current speeds must be removed, so mending compensations are required. As the fly drifts back downstream, the rod is elevated and the line-leader junction is above the surface. Rivet your attention on this, as the deeply sunken takes are short and subtle. If no strikes have occurred, permit the fly to continue downstream. Sometimes a fish will hit as the line tightens downstream and the fly responds by moving up off the bottom.

In very heavy, turbulent water a variation with a heavy sinking line, short leader and, a weighted stonefly numph works well. A short upstream cast is made, slack is recovered as needed, and once again as the fly passes your position the rod is well-elevated, then gradually lowered as the fly works on its downstream course. If anything, a slight influence on the fly helps; that is, the rod can lead the line as it comes downstream so the fish take solidly. Downstream and across a snappy, tip-jerking motion can bring the fly up towards the

Charles Loughridge working a deeply sunken nymph on a Colorado stream.

surface. Large stoneflies can scramble when they're disturbed, and strikes are hard.

Casts can also be directed across and downstream in choppy, boulder-studded water with a large nymph and the line type dictated by the depth of the water: a floater for near surface work, a sinktip or sinking line for deeper work.

Another effective time for nymphs is prior to and during an emergence of insects. There are dry fly parallels as a floating line and a single nymph usually work best. The fish are holding high in the water, visible to the angler, and can be approached with an up-and-cross stream cast. The line and perhaps the upper part of the leader should be well-greased. If the fish is easily visible, he should give an indication of the take. Or, watch closely where the leader penetrates the surface film and react to any sudden deviation from its normal drift. Should it stop, draw under the surface, or suddenly dart forward, it's a signal to strike quickly. Upstream dead drift methods when you're just covering the water, placing the nymph in likely feeding sites, or working with a longer line in difficult lighting conditions can be assisted by a strike detector of some kind. The innovative angler, Dave Whitlock, has popularized one method.

Razor the leader butt to a small, hairlike spike. Then, place this narrowed point through the eye of a needle. Cut a short section of bright orange fly line about one inch long and insert the needle right through this short section. With a pair of pliers draw the needle and monofilament through and then attach the leader to the line with your favorite nail or needle knot. You'll have a bright "indicator" that can ride against the knot and is very visible.

Some other approaches utilize cork or styrofoam as strike indicators and these seem to work well also. A few lines are now being made with brightly colored ends, but I've found that contrast obtained by a short indicator is best for me. Also, the Cortland Line Co. has recently introduced *Striker* (which sounds like a wonderfully appropriate name) and I've used this satisfactorily. It is a very visible tab with an adhesive back that can be pinched on the leader or line-leader junction. It is light weight and doesn't seem to interfere with casting or presentation. Finally, a bit of bright polypropylene yarn can be greased and tied in at the line-leader junction or on a leader knot.

Very often an emerger or floating nymph is effective. Depending on the stream, approaches are up and across, cross-stream slack-line casts, or down and across. If there is a singular fish which can only be approached from directly above, a slack line cast fed straight down may be productive as well.

The late Lew Oatman was a well-known subsurface fly expert who developed several popular streamers. On the lower Battenkill in Vermont and New York he often worked nymphs on long, cross-stream, slack line casts with telling effect.

The concept of streamer and bucktail fishing is baitfish simulation. Many anglers swim streamers and bucktails in early season or during rising water periods during the season and let it go at that. Yet, there is season-long effectiveness here as baitfish make up a goodly portion of the diet, especially

The ubiquitous sculpin is a favorite trout food and serves as the model for a number of effective fly patterns.

The Keel Fly concept can be very valuable, not only for surface flies, but various subsurface wets, nymphs, and streamers as well.

as fish become larger, more secretive, and devote less and less time to surface fedding. Streamer specialist Oatman contended that a great deal of the trout's diet in midsummer consisted of small fish. Many numphs matured during late spring and early summer and left the stream with very small numphs in their early instars, which resulted in the trout searching out small baitfish. He favored his Darter and Grizzly streamers on #8 and #10 long shank hooks and handled them in three basic variations. The first was to cast across stream and retrieve quickly, skittering the fly along near the surface in choppy and turbulent stream sections. the second method was to cast across and allow the fly to swing, moving the rod tip from side to side and recovering line in jerks and darts. In deep holes and placid stretches, the streamer was allowed to sink deep, twitched, and allowed to sink again in an attempt to suggest a wounded minnow that would roll, rest, and recover in a struggling way.

Another specialist, the late Larry Koller, contended the best single approach for the larger fish of his favorite Catskill waters was to cast just above and past the suspected lie of the trout, then retrieve rapidly with a high held rod to keep the fly well up towards the surface.

The Bucktail or a "looks like a lot of things muddler" can also be cast well upstream and across, and brought down in a combination of alternate dead drift and spasmodic twitching motion.

The dry fly is the favored method for most anglers. You can experience the thrill of seeing the strike. When no fish are showing and the angler is "searching" the stream, the usual approach is upstream and across near suspected cover and holding lies. If the fish are rising to a particular fly, any artifical should be close in shape, size, color, and manner of movement. Dries can also be fished in any direction. Cross-stream, slack-line casts, cross and downstream casts and even directly downstream floats are all effective. The real point of any method is to think about the best casting angle from which a cast can be accurately delivered, and to have the fly acting in a natural manner as it passes the fish.

Many anglers delight in studying aquatic life. Yet, all experienced anglers know very capable fishermen who know the difference between the various orders such as mayflies, stoneflies, caddis flies, etc. and more or less let it go at that. Without exception, however, these anglers are observant and respectful of the trout and his senses. They "match" the activity in the sense that if they see a cream colored, half inch long mayfly floating dead with the current, they select their fly on that basis. They may not be very concerned with the difference between *Ephemerella rotunda* and *Ephemerella invaria*, but they still catch fish. In effect, learning about aquatic life is valuable and interesting, but it is not always required for success.

As a starting point for the dry fly angler, it is best to have a variety of types. Most insects run to shades of gray, tan to brown, cream to ginger, and various olive hues. The quick, turbulent stream sections functionally call for high-floating, visible patterns, whereas the medium to slow currents require greater realism in shape, size, color and manner of movement. A basic starting point

54

Large Labrador Brook Trout that responded to "twitched" dry fly approach.

selection might include a few standard divided-wing patterns, no-hackle, and parachutes, a couple of sparse spiders or variants, midges and appropriate terrestrials. Add a couple of caddis imitations and perhaps a bivisible, hair-wing, or hair-body type for the quick stretches. Supplement these with locally popular flies, and there should be an appropriate fly type to deal with most requirements.

Finally, everyone who scribbles about the outdoors must resort to the inevitable cliché from time to time. I've never heard, for instance, of any outdoorsman taking to the trail, lifting the gun or fishing rod without first being duly fortified by "the hearty breakfast." The thought of heading out on nothing more than a piece of toast, juice, and coffee is apparently unthinkable. Another cliché is: **experiment!** When standard approaches don't work, try the offbeat: vary casting angles, retrieve speeds, depths, fly types; use bright attractor flies rather than the duller, more natural types; twitch and skim dries across the surface rather than dead drift them. The basic premise is always to feed the fish, but when that doesn't seem to work, some of the offbeat approaches may. So, even if it is a bit trite, do it: **experiment!**

6.

SPINNING

Spinning is a versatile and effective method that is well-suited to the desires of many backpacking anglers. The basics of equipment handling are learned more easily than is the case with either bait casting or fly fishing. However, this comparative ease is deceptive since expertise with spin gear, like any other method, ultimately demands complete familiarity with the equipment, its capabilities and limitations.

The backcountry spin angler has two general classifications of tackle to consider. Although various manufacturers devise their own descriptive nomenclatures, we can arbitrarily establish our own definitions.

The first, and most versatile, consideration would be a general purpose, light spin outfit geared primarily to one quarter ounce lures. In a standard, two-piece rod this typically consists of a six, six and a half, or seven foot model and a lightweight, open-faced spin reel spooled with four pound monofilament. Since there is no inertia to overcome at the beginning of the cast, such an outfit is fully capable of handling lures both lighter and heavier than one quarter ounce. Instinctively these specs suggest compatibility with medium to large streams as well as ponds and lakes. For many anglers there is no reason to look any further. On the other hand, while it's not really akin to burning down the forest to cook the turkey, such an outfit may be overcalibrated for some more specialized uses.

Some anglers delight in peeking and poking along the mini-creeks where delicately presented, tiny lures are called for. Even at low-water levels on larger streams the so-called ultra-lite approach may be most effective. Slightly scaled down versions of the standard gear are most productive then; sensitive sticks four and one half to six feet long, tiny reels spooled with two or three pound mono and lures of $\frac{1}{16}$ of an ounce, give or take a bit. The little reels can, of course, be spooled with heavier line on occasion, but basically this ultra-light outfit is for the little intimate waters and demands low water conditions on the larger streams.

At 6.5 oz. with a fast 5 to 1 retrieve ratio, the Orvis 50A spin reel handles lines from 2 to 6 lbs. test. Such a reel is well suited to the backpacker/angler.

The ultimate choice is an individual one depending on where and when you will be traveling. Some insight into equipment needs will surface as you do the pre-trip planning. You should have a good idea of the type and size of the streams and ponds you will encounter as well as their seasonal water levels.

There are a variety of rods to choose from with glass and graphite dominating the current market. Both materials make excellent spin sticks, but glass has the advantage of excellent knockabout durability at a lower cost. Both materials are available in standard, two-piece models as well as the occasional multi-sectioned, three- or four-piece models. There is also a relatively new five foot, five-piece glass rod with matching mini-size reel from Daiwa. This Daiwa *Minimite* system is expressly designed for the backpacking angler. It comes self-contained in a tough plastic case that is only about fifteen inches long. In spite of the five-piece breakdown, the action of the rod is surprisingly good. It handles a wide range of lure weights, including the one quarter ounce sizes, very well. It certainly deserves consideration from the backpacker looking for one outfit to cover a number of situations with a minimum of gear. In general the two-piece rods are standard, but the careful builder today can provide excellent multi-sectioned models that combine pleasing power to weight ratios, good handling characteristics and sensitivity. It wasn't too many years ago that, with a couple of notable exceptions, the multi-sectioned spin rods offered were worthless, insensitive as a tax collector, and more suited to pole vaulting than plugging. The disappointing aspect of many offerings was the fact that they often came from established firms with a historical significance that would indicate they should have known better. Fortunately, most of these have been redesigned; current pack spin rods are generally very good. To be on the safe side, check them carefully. Enlist the aid of a competent local dealer if you're unfamiliar with the feel of well-designed equipment.

In the standard, two-piece offerings of six to seven foot light rods, you will probably find satisfaction with a moderately fast action rod with most of the bend occuring near the tip. When selecting an ultra-light stick, try to find something a bit slower overall; that is, flexing a bit more into the butt section with a less pronounced tip action. The matching mini-lures used with this rod don't create much resistance to bend so the slower overall recoil characteristics are more desirable for casting ease and accuracy. In pack rod selection, be just as demanding of a good "feel." The use of a pack rod implies you are seeking as much convenience and versatility as possible from one outfit. With proper design and up-to-date ferrule arrangements, some of the pack rods have a feel virtually indistinguishable from a standard, two-piece rod. For all-purpose use, a pack rod that approaches a moderately fast action without undue butt section stiffness should do the job nicely.

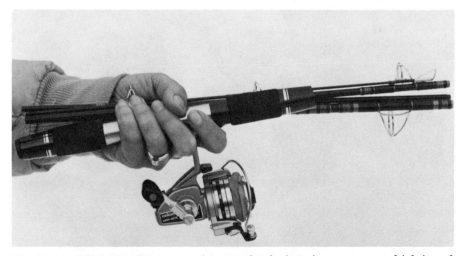

The Daiwa Minimite *System packs completely into its own case which is only about 15 inches long. The rod is a 5 foot, 5 inch piece model that has proven to be both convenient to pack and versatile in use.*

Casting

Casting with a spin outfit is a mechanical delight. The weight of the outgoing lure pulls line from the spool, and the spool remains stationary during the cast. Since there is no inertia to overcome at the beginning of the cast, the spin reel allows the use of very lightweight lures. As a result of this casting principle, the new angler may acquire the fundamentals of spin tackle handling in a fraction of the time required for equal facility with other methods such as a bait casting rod or even a fly rod.

The normal casting stroke is the overhand cast, useful at all times unless streamside obstructions dictate a different casting plane. The usual rod grip places the reel foot between the middle and ring fingers although the size of your hand may make a different placement more comfortable. The thumb lies along the top of the cork grip. The rod and forearm should be in a straight line, aimed at the desired target. The upper arm is comfortably close to, but not jammed tightly, against the body, Disengage the pickup bail with your free hand and lift the line free, supporting it on the ball of your index finger. Begin the casting stroke by smoothly pivoting off the elbow, lifting the casting hand to about eye level. When the forearm and rod reach a vertical position, stop. The weight of the lure flexes the rod to the rear. Bring the rod smoothly down and forward, reversing the original path traveled, releasing line as the rod approaches its starting position. There is a slight wrist emphasis at the top of

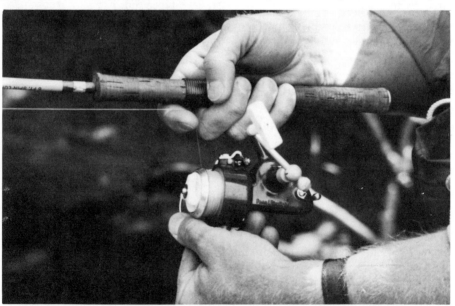

Support the line on the ball of the index finger. Open the bail in preparation for the cast.

the backstroke and at the end of the forward stroke.

About the only potential problem is the correct forward release point; releasing too early will send the lure sailing skyward, too late will sent it crashing into the water at your feet. A few trials and you'll be on the right track. You may, in fact, be pleasantly surprised when the lure sails out for excellent distance.

It's time now to face the reality of backcountry spinning. On the small to medium-sized streams, distance usually is not too important. Reasonable accuracy and lure control are more important. Backpacking and angling have enough inherent problems without introducing the need for tree climbing agility to retrieve artlessly flung lures dangling twenty feet above the pool in some ancient spruce tree. The key to accuracy and lure control is the index finger of the rod hand. With the lure in flight you can slow its speed to prevent overcasting the target by bringing the forefinger back towards the spool, creating

Bruce Bowlen demonstrates various casts

Aim the rod at desired target. Disengage the pickup bail and support the line on the ball of the index finger.

Pivot off the elbows, elevating the hand to the eye/ear level. Stop as forearm and rod attain the vertical. Lure weight flexes rod to the rear.

Reverse the original path with a smooth, fluid motion.

Line is released as the hand approaches the original, starting position.

friction against the outgoing line. The lure can be stopped completely by simply touching the spool rim with the forefinger. Spend some time in your practice sessions to ensure automatic responses from the index finger. It pays off in restricted quarters.

If streamside obstructions prevent the usual overhand casting stroke, work in sidearm or backhand planes. You can also use an underhanded tossing motion for moderate distance in very confined quarters. Still another possibility when really walled in is the bow and arrow cast. A cautious note accompanies the use of this cast: Be wary of those sharp hook points in preparing for and completing this cast.

Sidearm and backhand casts are practical when obstructions prevent the usual overhand stroke.

In really hemmed-in areas try the Bow and Arrow cast. Carefully grasp treble hooks and draw rod into circular bow. Lure-holding hand is about at a hip pocket level.

Then release lure, and cushion forward stroke by slightly elevating the rod hand as the lure begins its forward flight.

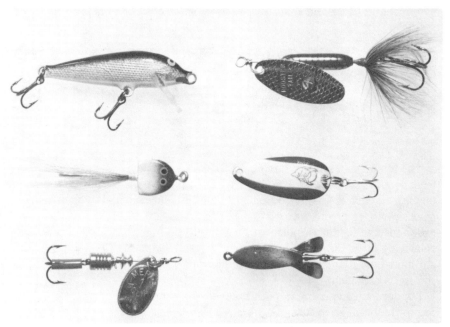

Representative Spinning Lure Types:

1. Rapala plug
2. Wiggle Jig
3. Mepps spinner
4. Rooster Tail Spinner
5. Red and White spoon
6. Swiss spinner

7.

BASIC FLY CASTING

Fly casting is mechanically less efficient than spinning. The spin lure represents a concentrated weight mass. As the spin rod swings forward the lure speeds on its way, pulling the trailing monofilament. In contrast, a fly is virtually weightless and cannot contribute to the cast. The burden of casting weight is in the fly line, distributed over those several feet of line extended beyond the rod tip. In effect, a spin lure makes the outgoing flight possible; a fly simply goes along for the outgoing ride, taken there by the unrolling and extending fly line.

Despite these differences, there are similarities in the basic casting strokes. Normal fly casting is relatively simple. There are only a few things to do right, everything else just complicates the learning process. The more practice sessions that can be arranged, the more rapid the progress. Assuming, of course, the correct motions are the ones that are practiced. The early sessions are best done on water if it is at all possible. The surface tension of water assists in the initial line-pickup motions. If water is unavailable, an open lawn will do almost as well. On moving water face downstream, strip off about twenty feet of line and allow it to drift downstream with the current. If practicing on the lawn select an open area of about forty or fifty feet. Stand in the middle as you require both backcast and forward cast space.

Throughout the discussions, the terms rod hand and line hand will be used so the instructions will be clear for both right-handed and left-handed casters. Initially, only the rod hand will be required. Begin by securing the fly line under the rod hand forefinger or hand itself, clamping it to the cork grip so it can't creep out. We want to work with a fixed line length for the moment. The premise is that the forearm, wrist, and hand will act primarily as a continuation of the rod through most of the casting cycle with the elbow as the major pivot point of the cast. The wrist will come into play briefly (but importantly) as a secondary pivotal point in both the top of the backcast and the end of the forward cast.

The grip on the corks should be comfortably firm with the thumb lying atop the grip, pointing down the rod. In the beginning sessions open up the rod side foot a bit. That is, a right-handed caster should stand facing the target area, the left foot facing straight ahead and placed slightly in advance of the right foot which is angled outward slightly, a position which permits turning the head easily to visually follow the rear line extensions of the backcast. Left-handers: reverse the procedure. The upper arm is close to the body, the elbow is separated from the body by a comfortable couple of inches. The forearm, wrist and hand now act as a continuation of the rod which is angled down slightly, the tip pointing toward the water. The stance is comfortable and the rod-side foot is sustaining most of the body weight.

The conventional cast is an overhand movement: Begin with a smooth, progressive, lifting motion, pivoting off the elbow with the wrist and hand held almost stiffly. This permits the entire rod to contribute effectively to the cast. With the short line you are working with, the end of the fly line and the upper part of the leader (butt section) may leave the water. Only the remainder of the leader is still in the surface film. Speeding up progressively, the hand raises toward eye level. As the rod approaches a vertical there is some wrist emphasis towards the rear. Tighten the squeeze on the grip with the thumb and index finger at this point and the rod should stop at the proper angle. The thumb is about vertical, or just slightly past vertical, and the rod is angled up and back. Turn your head to follow the rear line extension. Just before the unrolling "U" shape straightens out completely, begin the forward delivery of the cast.

In due time it won't be necessary to turn and watch the flow of the backcast; the feel and timing will become instinctive. However, most new casters learn to coordinate the timing of the movements easiest if they watch as well as try to feel the tugging line snuggling nicely against the rod in a proper backcast. The forward cast is a "path reversal." The forearm, hand and wrist are almost stiff and drive the rod butt progressively forward and down. As the rod starts to turn over in the front, the wrist and thumb come into play to emphasize the forward stroke. The cast is finished with the rod pointing straight ahead, just about parallel to the water. The line and leader should unroll completely in the air, extend fully and drop gently to the surface.

Try for smooth power application and the proper timing of the movements. Many new casters take extreme actions; some tend to handle the equipment too gently, thus failing to develop the required bend in the rod which will assist in obtaining the nice, flowing, back-and-forth motions of a good cast. Others try to overpower the equipment and apply strength in short, jerky bursts. Again, it's proper timing and smooth power application that will do the job most pleasantly and most efficiently.

Make this fundamental cast several times. Each one should be a complete

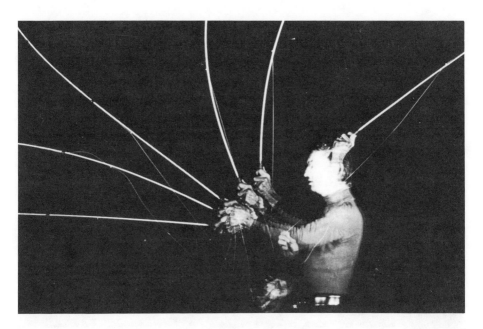

The average length, forward casting cycle in stroboscopic sequence. The hand is about at eye/ear level with the rod angled up and back of vertical. The hand pushes forward and down until a late wrist and thumb emphasis is introduced to bring the rod about parallel with the water.

cycle of pickup, backcast, forward cast, and delivery of the fly to the water. Try to make each cast better and smoother than the one previously. Rapid progress is possible if the practice sessions are handled correctly.

It is also important to realize the role of the backcast. New hands often minimize the importance of the backcast, placing most of their effort into the forward delivery. Nevertheless, if the backcast is properly formed, the forward cast is almost automatic. Tame the backcast first and everything else will fall into place quickly. Some find the concepts easier if they begin to work the rod in a sidearm motion, rather than overhead. Just alter the plane of the cast to a sidearm motion. The line loops will form and unroll more or less parallel to the ground. The line flow and the timing are easily watched and the importance of smoothly coordinated movements becomes quickly apparent. When this sidearming motion is under control, just change the angle of the cast, working back up into the normal overhead or vertical path.

The wrist is held almost stiffly through most, but not all of the motions. There is wrist emphasis at the top of the backcast and the end of the forward cast. The beginner's danger tends to be a slack wrist at the top of the backcast, angling the rod too far back, perhaps with the tip section pointed to the ground or water behind. Experienced hands say that the line follows the rod. What you do with the rod tip is reflected in the flow of the line a moment later. Therefore, watch the backcast and don't allow the rod to angle further back than it should. At the top of a well-delivered backcast, the rod hand is automatically placed in a position from which it is ready to drive forward into a nice delivery cast. The end of the forward cast is delivered with some wrist emphasis to bring the rod

The Basic Casting Cycle: (Landy Bartlett demonstrates) Begin the backcast by angling the rod low, with the tip pointing toward the water. Be sure to remove all slack line. Next, the forearm is elevated smoothly until only the leader remains on the surface of the water. This ensures the whole rod is lifting the line into the backcast. The line-holding hand simply maintains a light tension on the line.

At the top of the motion an easy wrist snap to the rear allows the line to flow up and back toward the required line extension. The casting hand is about at the eye/ear level and the line-holding hand is still maintaining light tension.

The original path is reversed as the casting hand drives smoothly and progressively forward and down to terminate in a decisive wrist and thumb power application. The line-holding hand is still maintaining tension. Some three feet of line exist behind it and lead to the fly reel.

The rod is stopped about parallel to the water. The unrolling fly line and leader will extend completely in the air and drop gently to the water. Note that the slack line that existed behind the line-holding hand is being allowed to shoot into the cast, pulled by the outgoing taper.

almost parallel to the water.

Another cast which helps to make the correct motions clear is the roll cast. Water is required for smooth execution of the roll cast. On the lawn the line tends to slide along ineffectually. Use the rod hand only, clamping the fly line to the cork grip so it can't creep out. It is vital to form this cast slowly, elevating the rod and tilting it slightly to the outside of the body so the rod and line lie in different planes and don't tangle on the forward cast portion of the cycle. A belly of line will form from the rod tip to the water. Allow this line belly to pass behind the elbow and come to a complete stop. Now, drive the rod hand ahead and down in a normal, forward casting motion, applying the casting power progressively and ending the cast with a short, decisive wrist and thumb power application. The rod should finish almost parallel to the water at the termination of the cast. About the only problems that may arise tend to do so for one of two reasons: first, the line must be brought into position quite slowly; secondly, the line must be allowed to stop for a brief second before the start of the forward stroke.

When these one-handed fundamentals are in good order, introduce the other hand, the line hand, to the movements. Even as a fundamental, the line hand role is very important, maintaining line control and tension. New casters tend to minimize its importance and are understandably fascinated by the rod motion. However, the line-hand role is vitally important to all fly casting. When advanced line hauling techniques become important, the line hand is just about as busy as the rod hand.

Strip an additional four or five feet of line from the reel and let it hang loosely from the butt guide, sagging back to the reel. Reach up to grasp the line between thumb and forefinger, letting the line lay loosely over the fingers. The line hand should now be at a comfortable distance to the side of the rod hand with the line coming directly from the butt guide to the hand under light tension. The belly of slack line now exists behind the line hand and sags back down and up to the reel. As the normal backcast is made, the line hand maintains light tension and is allowed to drift slightly across the body and up a bit, essentially following the path of the rod hand so that an equal distance between the hands is maintained during the whole cycle. On the forward delivery cast, the line can be fed through the line holding hand as the momentum of the outgoing taper pulls it for a slight extra shoot. Functionally, this line hand assures line control and maintains tension. Moving it to follow behind the rod hand places it in a position where it is available to introduce a well-coordinated pull of its own when the rod is coming forward to increase line speed and provide extra distance through the "shooting" of slack line. In a very real sense the line hand also aids accuracy in normal casting. If the line is fed consistently through the line hand, it is, as we've mentioned, under control. Closing the hand slightly when the line is on its outgoing forward flight slows the line somewhat. Pinching the line between the thumb and fingers stops the line over its target. Therefore, it is quite easy to cast with a bit more power than is required to reach a specific target area and then stop the line in flight over the designated area to drop the fly just where you want it.

The false casting cycle is a necessary procedure with multiple uses. Your accuracy is improved by lining up the flight of the line with the specific target

70

area. It dries a floating fly as excess water droplets are shaken from the fly during the back and forth motions. When coordinated with the line hand, false casts can help build up additional line speed to combat head winds or help shoot the line for extra distance. The procedure is essentially an incomplete forward cast. Stop the rod high on the forward stroke, as opposed to the parallel delivery cast position, and the line will begin to straighten in the air. Just before it reaches a complete forward extension, bring it back into another backcasting motion. When the delivery cast is to be made, allow the line to fully straighten to the rear. Catch it as the line weight snuggles against the rod and

The false cast is an incomplete forward casting motion, checked with the rod at a high angle, allowing the line to almost completely extend forward in the air before being brought back into another backcast. False casts allow you to get out more line without disturbing the water, and also dry off dry flies.

drive forward to finish with the usual smooth wrist emphasis and final rod turnover.

Although the usual stroke is overhead, that sidearm cast we looked at briefly is a valuable move on the stream. With shy fish we can often make close approaches by crouching and moving slowly and casting from a sidearm position to minimize the chance of the flashing rod being seen by the cautious trout.

An underpowered side-arm cast will produce a curve to the right as the line has insufficient power and speed to attain the normal straight line extension.

An overpowered side-arm cast, especially if it is checked abruptly by a vigorous throwing-in motion of the rod tip and assisted at the same time by a slight line-hand tug, will hook past a straight line extension and fall in a curve to your left.

Sidearm casts also help drive a fly under low hanging foliage. Furthermore, they allow modifications in our timing to introduce curves into the presentation. There are other curve cast methods, but the principle behind the curves is best understood if we examine the line flow of a sidearm cast. Any cast, no matter the angle of origin (overhead, sidearm, or backhand) extends in a straight line if the timing is correct. When casting sidearm, the line loops form more or less parallel to the water. A correctly executed cast extends forward in a straight line. However, if the forward stroke is underpowered, the line fails to attain the straight line and falls to the water in a curve to your right—if you are right handed. An overpowered sidearm cast, especially if it is checked abruptly in flight by a slight line hand tug, hooks around past our straight line and falls in a curve to the left.

Slack line casts are often advantageous to improve a float or drift, to contend with mixed and conflicting currents, or to work a fly directly downstream in such a manner that the fly moves with the current flow seemingly unrestrained by line or leader influence. One possibility is the "S" cast. This is formed by taking advantage of the fundamental that whatever is done to the rod during the cast will be reflected in the flow of the line a moment later. Allow the backcast to straighten to the rear in the normal manner. As the rod moves into the forward stroke, wiggle it from side to side. The line passing through the guides is influenced by the side-to-side rod movements and extends and drops onto the water in a series of wiggles or "S" shapes. This action can be controlled easily be varying the number and size of the curves that are formed. A few firm, widely spaced wiggles of the rod produce a few deep curves; a series of quicker, shorter, side-to-side rod movements produce a larger number of smaller curves.

There are some alternative motions to introduce slack into the cast. To keep much of the slack near the fly, make the cast with insufficient power to fully straighten out. This is actually a slightly underpowered normal cast. Some casters prefer a forward stroke made with greater emphasis than is needed to reach the target. At the end of the forward motion a slight pull back is made. This causes the speeding line to bounce back and drop in a series of slack curves. Still another alternative is the parachute cast. On the final forward delivery start the rod ahead and stop it abruptly while it is still vertical. Don't follow through on the forward stroke. The rod hand moves from a position opposite your ear straight ahead for about eighteen inches; then it is abruptly checked. Immediately lower the rod hand about a foot and the incomplete forward stroke will yank the line and leader backward. It will fall loosely to the water. On a direct downstream drift, the rod can then be brought to a position parallel to the water and more line can be pulled from the reel and shaken out of the guides to extend a long drift.

The cast with the greatest distance potential is the double haul. Despite the fact that you will be attempting longer distance casts, the key elements remain smoothness and proper timing of the rod hand and line hand. Since there are more motions involved, practice with more than the usual amount of line extended beyond the rod tip.

Lay out some thirty five or forty feet of line. Strip another twenty feet of line from the reel and allow it to drop loosely at your feet. The grip on the rod is a bit firmer than usual. Lean forward a little to extend the line hand towards the butt or first guide and grasp the line firmly between the thumb and forefinger. Begin moving the line towards you a split second before the rod begins to lift. This starts the line moving towards you and helps to power the line into a smooth backcast. The hands now work in opposing directions: The line hand sweeps down and back heading for a hip pocket position, while the rod hand moves up and back towards a strong backcast position. The hands are momentarily separated. Now, as the backcast begins to extend to the rear, the line hand (still holding the line in the same relative position) moves up and across the body towards the rod hand. With the backcast straight out behind the rod, the line hand starts a smooth accelerating movement back towards the hip pocket position and the rod hand drives ahead. A decisive wrist and thumb delivery complete the rod turnover and the line hand releases its grip on the line. The outgoing taper pulls the extra slack through the guides for a long forward line extension.

If the single cycle isn't enough to gain the desired distance or line speed, simply false cast a time or two and then release the line for the final shoot.

Although the double haul is definitely the big water, long distance cast, the principle is valuable with any tackle. On small streams just a slight tug of the line hand helps overcome the surface tension and move the line into a nice backcast. A tiny pull with the line hand while coming forward can shoot a line for extra yardage or help compensate for a sudden puff of headwind.

The double haul can be done with the double taper or the weight forward line, but many anglers who must habitually reach way out prefer the shooting head. This is a short, usually thirty foot fly line section, attached to one hundred feet of twenty to twenty-five pound monofilament or a specially made small diameter level fly line. Conventional backing line fills the remainder of the reel. Anglers working with shooting heads have devised some unique methods of handling the loose running line behind the "head." Some rig paper clips or clothespins to their wader tops on which to hang the coils. Some hold the loose coils in their mouth and open their mouth on the forward cast to let the line soar away. Some anglers prefer the shooting basket to handle the retrieved line, stripping it into the basket to be shot forward on the subsequent cast.

From the standpoint of handling the head while casting, there are two points worthy of mention. Keep the shooting head close to the rod tip. If the head is too far from the rod tip, the light monofilament cannot support it properly. If it is too close to the rod tip, the connection between the head and the mono may be pulled into the tip top and interfere with the smoothness of the motions. Work with it a while to find the correct overhang for you. Usually something between two and six feet is appropriate. Next, on the final forward stroke release the cast earlier or aimed higher than normal since there is less friction in the guides to slow its flight. It will turn over too fast otherwise.

The wind is an obvious fact of angling. It can come at you from any angle. When it's brisk enough, it must be compensated for.

With a strong wind from the rear, it's best to begin with a strong horizontal line pickup supplemented by a short, smooth line-hand pull. The rod angle is essentially the same as employed in a usual sidearming cast which keeps the line low where there may be less wind resistance. Turn your head to watch the unrolling loop. As it straightens, immediately start a looping overhand forward stroke. There is no pause in the whole cycle. The backcast and forward cast planes are widely separated and there is no danger of them tangling. The line weight nestles continuously against the rod and the whole motion is a smooth, continuous oval which starts to the side and sweeps up and overhead with the forward cast aimed higher than normal to take advantage of the following wind.

The on-coming headwind is only a problem of velocity. There's no problem in getting a smooth backcast as it is wind assisted. The key to defeating or contending with the headwind lies in a smooth, strong, accelerating forward delivery. A line hand pull at the time the rod turns over helps throw a tight, narrow loop into the wind. The rod turnover is delayed as long as possible. The idea is to keep the line driving tight and close to the water.

Crosswinds offer the potential hazard of having the fly driven right at you. Ideally the rod is always on the downwind side. If, for example, you are right handed, the wind that blows from left to right is no problem. Everything is safely away from your body. the wind crossing from right to left is more dangerous. Compensations may depend on the wind velocities. If the breezes aren't too strong and gusty, a strong sidecasting motion will probably be sufficient. Stronger winds call for different measures. One possibility is to alter the normal casting planes. If you are righthanded, make the backcast with the rod tilted away slightly to the right and keep the rod hand high as the backcast unrolls to the rear. As you come forward alter the plane of the forward stroke and bring your hand virtually overhead. The line will ride high and pass safely to your left. Or, use the backhand cast. Start by holding the rod in the usual manner, but angled toward the downwind side. That is, a righthanded caster with a wind blowing from right to left would angle the rod across the body and to the left. The pickup is made off the elbow, assisted by a short line-hand tug. The rod angles up over your left shoulder. The backcast unrolls safely downwind and you are ready for the forward stroke. Move ahead with the usual stiffish forearm drive, assisted by the ending wrist and thumb emphasis. A smooth line-hand tug on the forward cast will help pull in extra speed if it is needed.

There are some variations of the usual line pickup that can be helpful on the stream. The norm is a smoothly accelerating motion up and back. With a long line extended, a short line-hand pull helps to coordinate with the lifting rod to power into the firm and decisive backcast that's needed. Apart from these usual considerations there are a couple other possibilities. One is the roll cast pickup. Dry fly anglers normally face the current and work the fly back close to their position. The roll pickup saves time and is very easy to execute. As the line

The Roll Cast permits a forward line extension when the caster is hemmed in by obstacles to the rear. Begin by slowly elevating the rod, tilting it slightly to the outside of the body so the rod and line lie in different planes and won't tangle on the forward cast portion of the cycle. A belly of line will form from the rod tip to the water. Allow this to pass behind the elbow and come to a complete stop. Then, drive the rod hand ahead and down in a normal casting motion, applying the casting power smoothly and progressively and ending with a decisive wrist and thumb power application. The rod should be about parallel to the water at the termination of the cast. Be sure that the line is brought into position slowly, and allow the line to stop momentarily before beginning the forward cycle.

The roll cast pickup is commonly employed by upstream-directed anglers. It is also useful with sinking lines and shooting heads to lift these airborne with a minimum of fuss. As the belly of slack forms outside the rod-side shoulder, briskly snap the rod forward with an incomplete roll casting motion. The moving loop will pick line, leader and fly off the water and into the air, where a standard backcast can be made.

---

drifts back, elevate the rod slowly, tilting it outside and allow the line loop to form outside your elbow. Start the rod forward but do not follow through. Stop the rod with the butt angled about 45° above the water. A moving loop forms to pick line, leader, and fly off the water and into the air. Now a normal backcasting motion can be made. This pickup also works very well with sinking lines and shooting heads.

The snap pickup accomplishes much the same thing as the roll pickup. Bring the rod towards an eleven o'clock position. Then make a quick wrist snap, stopping the rod at about ten o'clock. A running curve moves down the line and kicks the fly upward and into position for the backcast. This lifting pickup, as opposed to one that draws the line across the surface, is very useful in avoiding obstructions or surface weeds. The fly doesn't have to be drawn into the weeds where it may hang up.

The switch or zig-zag pickup is one more way to avoid obstacles. This motion forces a series of moving curves into the line to lift the fly into the air. Hold the rod forward, angled slightly down toward the water. Then move the rod firmly from side to side while you elevate the arm. By the time the rod tip is between ten and eleven o'clock the fly should have left the surface and a normal backcast can be made.

When you are actually fishing, the forefinger of the rod hand will act almost as another rod guide. After the cast settles on the water, you want to be in a correct position to strike the fish. Most anglers place the line over the forefinger of the rod hand or between thumb and forefinger of the rod hand. All retrieves or line manipulations are done behind this grip to assure a quick, slack free response to a taking fish. There are a number of retrieve variations. The easiest is to form coils of line in the line hand. Gather in the first loop well back in the hand. Place the next loop slightly forward of this. Hold the last gathered loop in place by the thumb and forefinger. Line can be released to an outgoing cast in an orderly manner without snags.

Generally speaking, fish should be played off the reel. Small fish are sometimes just stripped in, but all desirable fish demand being handled off the reel. If there is a great deal of slack when the fish takes, it can be slipped under the index finger of the rod hand as the fish makes his initial run while, at the same time, the balance of the slack line is being reeled in. With all the slack taken up, the rod is elevated and the fish goes where he will, but runs off the reel. When you can recover line, do so by reeling in.

Netting a tired fish isn't difficult. Unfortunately, they often have something left. Many a fish has been lost at this last critical moment. Submerge the net and bring the fish in head first. If the head of the trout is held high, he won't see the net. Then slack the line so the fish will naturally turn into the net meshes and lift him free.

8.

EQUIPMENT COVERAGE

Fly Lines

To lay the groundwork for any fly line discussion, we should get the terminology in order and comprehend the current line rating system. Since 1961 a fly line rating based on weight has been in effect. The weight factor around which the system revolves is the grain: $437\frac{1}{2}$ grains equal one ounce. The committee from the American Fishing Tackle Manufacturers Association which formulated the ratings further concluded the average length cast to be 30 feet, so the system is concerned only with the first 30 feet of line, exclusive of any taper tip. The grain weights for various lines were given numerical designations from 1 through 12 (although some special purpose heavier lines have since come into being), and the weights range from 60 grains (a #1 line) to 380 grains (a #12 line) plus or minus acceptable manufacturing tolerances. Prefixes were established to designate taper type: L for level line; DT for double taper; WF for weight forward; and ST for single taper or shooting head. Letters indicate line function: F for floating line; S for sinking line; I for intermediate, a line which has a specific gravity about that of water. When dressed the intermediate line can serve as a floating line. Without treatment it serves as a slow sinking line. Lastly, F/S indicates a floating-sinking type such as the popular sinktip lines where the 10 feet of line at the end sinks while the balance of the line floats. There are other versions of this concept with 20 or 30 foot forward sinking sections.

When taken in combination, the system tells us taper type, weight and function, e.g., DT5F is a double taper 5 weight (140 grains) floater, a WF5S is a weight forward 5 weight (140 grains) sinking line and a WF5F/S would be a weight forward 5 weight (140 grains) floating-sinking line in which the forward section of the line sinks while the balance floats.

There is rarely any need for the average angler to be concerned with the actual grain weights. The simple numerical designations are usually adequate information. About the only confusion that may arise occurs when looking at the sinking lines. Available technology permits the line makers to vary the specific gravity of the line coatings to achieve differing sink rates from quite slow to very fast. Since the AFTMA ratings do not take this into account, the manufacturers further identify their various sinking lines by labeling the product with an indication of the relative sinking speed. For example, the Cortland Line Company offers their Type 1 slow sinker, Type 2 fast sinker, Type 3 extra fast sinker and their Type 4 super sinker. Another leading line manufacturer, Scientific Anglers, varies the terminology but also offers sinking lines of four densities. Beyond this there are some special cases where a lead core line may be set up as a shooting taper system for really deep work. About all we can tell at the moment is that a specific line from a given maker will sink slower or faster than a different sinking line from the same maker. Perhaps in time there will be a specific standard established, but in truth the lack of such a standard is no hindrance. The line makers identify the relative sinking rates, and the specific gravity information is usually available. There's no problem in sorting out the suitable sinking line for your requirements.

Despite some specialized loose ends, the line rating system supplies the essential information and greatly simplifies line-to-rod relationships. Virtually all rod makers indicate the recommended line weights to use. What remains is the question of function and taper type. For most anglers the first fly line should be a floater. Which then, double taper or weight forward? Within the framework of their design, both are good. The double taper is reversible: As one end wears it can be swapped end for end to provide long term economy. At short and medium distances the double taper does well everything asked of it, be it roll casting, delicate presentation, or whatever. But, the arguments go, so does a well-designed forward taper. Some makers in fact run tapers that are identical for the first 30 feet so there is little to choose between the two line types where these average requirements are concerned. However, let's say it is necessary to present a fly quickly to a more distant target. You're working with 30 feet of line in the air and a good fish suddenly shows at the 50 foot distance. With a weight forward line the effective pulling weight is out there, beyond the rod tip. When the line is shot on the delivery cast, this advancing, pulling weight tugs along a lighter weight, smaller diameter running line.

By comparison, a double taper with a 30 foot working length of line in the air would be asked to pull a heavier, larger diameter, belly section out of the guides. Thus, the pulling weight of a double taper has more of a frictional load and a greater line weight to overcome. It's also likely that there will be less line speed obtained in a minimum of motions with the double taper, so the caster must apply more power to the cast or work through one or two additional false cast motions.

LINE RATING
SYSTEMS

Symbols

L	=	Level
DT	=	Double Taper
WF	=	Weight Forward
ST	=	Single Taper

Weights

#	Wt.	Range
1	60	54 — 66
2	80	74 — 86
3	100	94 — 106
4	120	114 — 126
5	140	134 — 146
6	160	152 — 168
7	185	177 — 193
8	210	202 — 218
9	240	230 — 250
10	280	270 — 290
11	330	318 — 342
12	380	368 — 392

Types

F = Floating
S = Sinking
I = Intermediate (Floats or Sinks)
F/S = sink tip

Weight in grains based on first 30′ of line exclusive of any taper tip:

Examples:

DT9S

Tip ◄———30 ft. 240 grains

DT9F

Tip ◄———30 ft. 240 grains

(Note: 437½ grains equal 1 ounce)

Chart: Courtesy
Orvis Co., Inc.

Profiles and taper dimensions of selected Cortland 333 Tapered lines.

CORTLAND "333" DOUBLE TAPERS

DT6F   6"   8'   73' Belly   8'   6"

DT8F   6"   8'   73' Belly   8'   6"

DT9F   6"   8'   73' Belly   8'   6"

CORTLAND "333" ROCKET TAPERS

WF5F   6"   12'   18' Belly   6'   68½' Running Line

WF7F   6"   12'   20' Belly   6'   66½' Running Line

WF8F   6"   12'   24' Belly   6'   62½' Running Line

WF9F   6"   16'   26' Belly   6'   56½' Running Line

Chart: Courtesy Cortland Line Co.

Another everyday fact of angling life is wind. The weight distribution of the forward taper is a more favorable distribution to contend with such conditions. An overly brief consensus then concludes that when the fishing is done on small, sheltered waters where delicate presentation is the usual requirement, the economy of a double taper is an influencing factor. However, if you need, as many do, the versatility to handle many different circumstances, the weight forward is apt to make the most sense.

The backpacking angler must be weight and space conscious when assembling an outfit. The usual procedure is to select a rod, then a reel and line to go with it. Working backwards in outfit assembly is a more satisfactory arrangement in that it keeps the emphasis on the appropriate line weight. Realistically, the fly size range to be presented determines the leader tippet size, while the physical conditions such as average required casting distance, water clarity, etc., help determine leader length. Then the fly line is the delivery vehicle to carry the fly and help kick the leader over neatly. This line must be of an appropriate weight to satisfy the twin demands of handling the average distance needs and reasonable fly presentation. The rod should be selected by its ability to move the selected line weight efficiently and comfortably. Since virtually every region of the country that offers potential interest to the angler-packer offers a range of possible water types from small sheltered waters up to larger rivers and lakes, versatility is important.

No single outfit does everything equally well. Therefore, a quick look at the inherent functional qualities of various line weights may help establish the best starting point for the individual angler. The very lightweight tapers such as #3 and #4 are ideally suited to small fly presentation over wary fish in demanding conditions. Being so light, however, they may be difficult to handle in the wind. As good as they are for their purpose, they must be regarded as fairly specialized. A #5 weight approaches the better compromise ground, as it expands the range of fly sizes that may be handled easily without sacrificing much in the way of delicate presentation when it's needed. Though it is not the best line weight for beating the breezes or really consistently long casts, it has enough weight to reach a good distance in the hands of a moderately competent caster. The #6 weight is capable of excellent fly presentation and the bonus of a bit more line weight further expands the fly size range and distance potential. There are many anglers who regard this as the line for one rod use. The #7 weight is enough line to handle nicely under breezy conditions. It handles an excellent range of fly sizes and types. Admittedly it's a bit more line weight than one would like for extremely spooky trout in demanding conditions when tiny flies are required, but it is an excellent all purpose line for medium to larger streams and most ponds and lakes. This weight is especially popular in many western areas as the starting point, general purpose trout line. Stepping up to the heavier 8, 9 and 10 weight lines is an implication that the emphasis is on larger flies, large water requirements, and perhaps longer average casting requirements or deeply sunken work with big wets, nymphs, streamers, and bucktails.

Based on this, the starting point for most backpacking anglers will fall in the middle range from the lightish #5 line through the medium weights of 6 and 7. There are so many variables that these suggestions should be modified or reinforced by expert local advice. Your local dealer can discuss your intentions knowingly, and being familiar with the area water types and seasonal imitative problems, he can help you zero in on the specific line weight and corresponding outfit.

On an everyday basis, the angler may head for the stream with a reel and an extra spool rigged with a different line type, or he may even carry two reels fully loaded and ready to interchange quickly. The "spare" equipment weight isn't a consideration in conventional day to day angling. However the backpacker has special problems and is very conscious of weight and space. If it's a weekend trip into a backwoods pond, the overall pack weight shouldn't be excessive. The angler might get by with a reel and an extra spool rigged with a different line type. Longer trips or trips into areas where there is a variety of water types present more problems. The weight of extra reels or even extra spools with all the line types that one might like to have along can be excessive. Fortunately, there is an answer: the shooting taper system.

The typical shooting taper is a short, usually 30 foot, length of fly line which is attached to 100 feet of monofilament or lightweight, small diameter level fly line. This in turn is attached to conventional dacron or micron backing which fills the balance of the reel spool.

The concept is valuable enough for any angler to at least consider for everyday work, but for the backpacking angler it is vital if maximum versatility is to be obtained with a minimum of weight and pack space. The hiker could, for instance, take off to the mountains with a single fly reel and several 30 foot shooting heads such as a floater, a sinktip, a slow sinker, a fast sinker, and an extra fast sinker and still have the whole arrangement weigh less and take up less space than a fly reel with one extra spool. And no matter at what level the fish were working, there would be an appropriate line type available to reach them.

Many shooting heads are available commercially. They can also be easily made up. Cut a conventional fly line 30 feet back from the end. It's most economical to cut a double taper, as two tapered heads and one level head will be obtained. Perhaps an angling buddy will go in on the price of a double taper, giving each of you a tapered head. You can flip a coin for ownership of the level head that remains.

Most commercial heads come with a spliced-in attaching loop. If monofilament is used behind the head, it is commonly clinch-knotted to this loop. To change heads, simply cut the knot and tie on the next head that is to be used. With level fly line you need to splice in a loop. This is connected to the shooting head in a loop to loop junction to form a square knot. To change heads, just unloop the one and loop on the next. These interlocking loops are also used to connect the running line to the backing. They are strong, smooth, and reliable. Your dealer may be able to splice any needed loops, although it's an easy

FOR ATTACHING FLY TO LEADER . . . .

The Clinch Knot

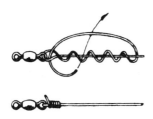

1. Thread line through eye.
2. Give line at least five turns around itself, then bring end back through the loop.
3. While holding line end, pull the twists tight up against the eye.

TO MAKE LOOP FOR ATTACHING
LEADER BUTT TO FLY LINE . . . .

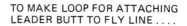
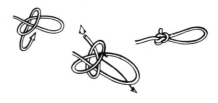

The Perfection Knot

1. Take 1-1/2 turns around the line.
2. Bring end through between the forward and back loops of turn taken in Step 1.
3. The back loop formed in Step 1 is then pulled up through the front loop, and pulled tight.

The Turle Knot

1. Thread leader through eye of fly. Then holding an open loop, tie a "Granny" Knot, forming a sliding loop.
2. Bring open loop forward over the fly.
3. Pull on leader 'til loop closes, tight behind the eye of the fly.

TO CONNECT THE SECTIONS OF A
TAPERED LEADER . . . . .

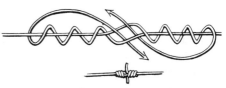

The Barrel Knot

1. Give end of line 1 at least three turns around line 2, and bring end back through loop as illustrated.
2. Give end of line 2 same number of turns around line 1 (in reverse rotation) and bring back through loop (in opposite direction).
3. While holding both line ends, pull twists firm and tight against each other. Ends can be trimmed very close, giving a neat smooth knot.

Basic Fisherman's Knots

procedure and worth doing yourself. One standard reference for this type of information as well as all other angling knots is *Practical Fishing Knots* by two fine angler-authors, Lefty Kreh and Mark Sosin (Crown Publishers, New York).

Behind the shooting head itself there are three possibilities: flattened or oval monofilament, round monofilament, or small diameter level fly line. The flattened mono floats well and may tangle less in normal use than the round mono, but it is susceptible to kinking or twisting. The round mono is very durable and forming knots is slightly easier than in the oval mono, but it may tangle more often. Both types of mono should be kept clean for best handling and longest casting qualities. The use of a silicone conditioner such as *Mono-Slik* from Maxima is recommended. The flotation of the mono will be improved and twist and drag will be reduced. The alternative to either monofilament is a small diameter line marketed as shooting line or the purchase of a lightweight, small diameter level fly line such as a L2F. For the beginner with the shooting head concept, this may be the best arrangement. The casting distance is reduced but the handling qualities of the level fly line are easier for the beginner to adjust to than the use of monofilament.

In any case, behind this 100 foot length of mono or level fly line, the balance of the reel space is taken up by conventional backing line, usually of 20 pound test.

Anytime there's an extensive backpacking-angling trip ahead where there may be a variety of water types calling for a variety of approaches, the shooting taper system is the lightweight, space saving, and versatile way to go.

Fly Rods

At the mention of backpack fishing, most people visualize one of two general situations. The first is the image of small brushy streams and backwoods ponds. The other is the high ponds and lakes of the western mountain regions. Certainly these are within the scope of the backpacking angler, but there is considerably more latitude than these possibilities. Some judicious searching in virtually any area of the country that offers fair to good trout fishing reveals a wide variety of possibilities for the angler willing to get off the beaten paths. These encompass every conceivable water type and size.

No single rod is always appropriate. In fact I can't think of a single, long term, serious, fly rodding acquaintance who owns only one fly rod. In the normal course of expanding experience, various rods are acquired to best suit variable seasonal or water type requirements. Yet, there should be a reasonably versatile starting point that doesn't compromise too much in the dual requirements of a gentle fly delivery or comfortable handling of the average casting distance requirements. Taken on a nationwide basis, the best selling fly line weight is a number 6, which is a reasonable compromise for the average backpacker. It's enough line weight to cast well and handle a range of fly sizes and types, but it is still light enough to present a fly gently in demanding presentation circumstances. There are any number of fly rods calibrated to swing in phase with a 6 weight line. They vary considerably in material, price, length, and number of rod sections.

Although there are some other possibilities peeking over the horizon, the general availability of materials at this time includes bamboo, boron-graphite blends, graphite, and fiberglass. For average use all of them can be excellent, and all of them can be considerably less than excellent. Material itself is only a starting point of potential. The designed taper establishes the action or feel, and a number of manufacturing variables further influence how well that inherent potential of a material is exploited and translated into user satisfaction. A great deal of the current rod advertising is material oriented. Obviously material is important, but the fact remains that how a material is handled in design, taper, and manufacturing always has been, and will remain, of at least equal importance.

For average use, most rod builders feel a beginning point fly rod should exhibit a smoothly progressive loading ability with the whole rod capable of contributing nicely to the cast. This medium taper should enable the user to handle a short, accurate line nicely, and exhibit the ability to reach well out when a longer line is called for.

That final material choice is elusive and to some extent may be price dependent. In general, bamboo is the most expensive choice, followed by graphite-boron combinations, then graphite, and fiberglass at the lower end of the price range. Each material has its adherents. They all have some appeal for segments of the buying public's taste and preference. For backpacking use, bamboo is the

Vivian Shohet of The Bamboo Rod, Weston, Vermont, manufactures his Green Mountain Backpacker *bamboo rod in two versions: a 7 ft., 4 piece model for lines 4 and 5, and another 7 ft., 4 piece version for lines of 6 and 7 weight. Many offerings of the pack rod concept are available in graphite and glass for packing ease.*

minority material. It is the most expensive and occupies the minor volume segment of the market anyway. Still, some anglers prefer this traditional material to all other alternatives. Graphite has come a long way in a few short years. The early problems of ferrule breakage and overall durability are virtually eliminated. Further, the tapers and actions have improved, and there is a wide choice of rod lengths and a greater availability of three piece long rods that are convenient to pack. Glass has a thirty year technology and design. Despite the "press" that newer materials are receiving, glass is an excellent value that should not be overlooked, especially if price is a consideration.

The length of the rod and the number of sections are as elusive and personal as the choice of material from which the rod is made. I could name several well known anglers with a basic agreement on what line weight is functionally suited to a particular piece of water, but the rod they choose to swing to support that same line weight varies by a full 3 feet—from 6 to 9 feet. To further complicate the matter, each of these anglers could come up with a reasonably plausible explanation to justify their particular choice. The short rod advocate delights in the intimate feel of the little sticks. He believes he has a greater "feel" for the casting, hooking, and playing of the fish. In windy conditions he feels he's able to keep the line low and close to the water. With his stiff, fast-tipped rod he can fire a neat, tight loop, almost under the wind as it were. A long rod advocate counters by pointing out his own sense of control. He can pick a longer line off the water nicely, avoid sagging backcasts into streamside brush, and he can guide the drift of the fly and make any line mending corrections more easily.

Since the go-light guy or gal needs as much versatility as possible, let's look at a couple of other options. In addition to the straightforward concept of the pack rod, there are some combination rods worth consideration: the fly-spin possibility or the spin-fly possibility. Again, it's a matter of limited availability in bamboo with more offerings available in graphite or fiberglass. And there are various ways of handling the concept. If the emphasis is on fly rod function and using a spin reel as an accommodation, the makers start with a standard fly rod blank. Then, the individual approach is varied. Some makers utilize a long, level, cork grip and sliding reel bands which accommodate the fly reel in its conventional rear of the grip location, and permit repositioning in mid-grip for the spin reel. The first one or two guides are sometimes slightly oversized to help funnel down the spiraling spin line.

Each angler has creditable arguments, but I'd have to advise the newcomer to avoid each extreme. Short, light rods are a delight. A quick appraisal of their characteristics, however, indicates that they are better in the hands of the experienced angler, for timing and casting smoothness are more critical if they are to perform at their maximum. The very long rods may be a nuisance in confined quarters even though the arguments of line control and mending ease are still valid. Also, if one is consistently wading deep or working out of a float tube, extra rod length is helpful. Presumably our theoretical backpacking angler will be fishing a variety of waters through the course of a usual season.

*For the one-rod backpacking angler, the combination fly/spin concept is popu-
lar. Sliding reel bands permit positioning of the spin reel in mid-grip or
mounting the Orvis CFO reel further back in the conventional location.*

Extremes in rod length at either end should be avoided.

In double-checking some preferences for our hypothetical #6 rod, I've consulted a number of anglers and rod building friends. The averages come out about like this: In bamboo, the most popular length is $7\frac{1}{2}$ feet, followed by 8 feet, then 7 feet; in glass, the most popular is an 8 foot model, closely and almost equally followed by $8\frac{1}{2}$ feet and $7\frac{1}{2}$ feet; in graphite, the 8 foot, $8\frac{1}{2}$ foot and 9 foot lengths for a 6 weight line are almost equally popular. There were quite a few who qualified this latter observation by saying that anglers working open rivers and ponds were tending toward the 9 foot for 6 as their first choice.

Most middle range fly rods handle at least a couple of line sizes with reasonable satisfaction. The best rod designs aim at a particular line weight, but because of line weight distribution (double taper versus weight forward and shooting tapers trailed by very light running lines, plus rod taper design and material characteristics) there is quite a bit of versatility inherent in most models. For example, if your rod handles 35 or 40 feet of a double taper 6 without any problem, it's bound to handle one belly size larger in a weight forward (a #7). Since the weight-aware backpacker is in need of versatility, I'd suggest you try your current fly rod with a line size lighter than recommended as well as a line size heavier than recommended, particularly in weight forward and shooting tapers. You may find you're able to customize to some extent to contend with differing circumstances.

The two piece rods are the most popular, and a two piece 8 foot rod isn't at all hard to pack. If you're up into a 9 foot graphite rod, then you might look for a three piece model for extra convenience. Modern ferruling methods can be so good you'll never notice any functional difference in performance, and the transport of the rod is somewhat easier. Some backpackers contend that only a true pack rod of 3 to perhaps 5 pieces is worth consideration because of transport ease. I doubt this is a really valid observation. Probably ninety percent of all the backpacking done by the angler is on trails, and even if rather extensive bushwhacking or off-trail travel is to be done, this is not an automatic assumption that the travel will be tough. Some areas are open and easy to travel. When the going is through tough brush, you'll have your own bulk and that of the pack to contend with. I can't see that the minor addition of a rod case taped alongside the frame will make a great deal of difference in travel ease. In other words, if you don't own a pack rod, just take along whichever rod you own that's capable of doing the job at the destination.

If you do prefer the pack rod concept, there are a number from which to select: a few in bamboo, more still in graphite and fiberglass. As I've hinted at previously, the fact that a rod breaks down into multiple sections should not imply a lessening of performance. You have a right to expect good performance. The quality rod builder can make these multi-sectioned models almost indistinguishable from the more standard two piece models. There's no question they are very convenient to pack.

Another common approach uses a reversible handle, set one way for fly reel use, reversed for spin reel use. This also works. Beyond the fact that the concept exists, how does it perform? Actually, quite well. The fly rod usage should feel normal as the blank is a normal fly rod taper. A fly rod blank set up in this manner is a good light spin option. On the assumption that you'll be using a small spin reel to begin with, with a none too large spool diameter, there is no real problem in funneling the spinning line through the guides. I have one especially hardheaded friend who swears by such a rig. His prejudices include sinking lines, despite any number of lectures. He uses a graphite fly-spin rod with a floating fly line. He lengthens leaders and adds twist ons for some subsurface work, but if the fish are lying deep, he just switches to an ultra-light spin reel. His results are excellent, and perhaps, more importantly, he finds it fun. That is difficult to argue with.

The flip side of the coin is the angler who is primarily a spin fisherman and would like to use a fly occasionally. The starting point is a spin blank set up to accommodate this occasional fly line usage. To illustrate the concept, there is one (of multiple offerings) from Fenwick. Their SF74-4 is a 7 foot pack rod with a recommended spin lure weight range from $\frac{1}{8}$ to $\frac{3}{8}$ ounces, using 2 through 6 pound monofilament. Or, it can carry a #6 fly line instead. The rod weight is $4\frac{3}{4}$ ounces, the pack length is 24 inches and when it's in its carrying case there is a total pack weight of 14 ounces.

If the concept of such versatility is appealing but at present you only own a fly rod or a spin rod, don't despair. Take the fly rod out in the yard with an ultra-light spin reel. You can mount it in the normal fly reel location (but I'd suggest you try taping it to the mid-portion of the cork grip). Try lures from about $\frac{1}{8}$ to $\frac{1}{4}$ ounce in trial casts. Due to the usual taper differences between a fly rod and a standard spin rod, you'll find the casting stroke slower; but, overall the concept can work out fine, and it can bring another possible approach to your go-light travels. In some areas this is a fairly routine practice. Mickey Powell at Buz's Fly and Tackle in Visalia, California has mentioned that several backpackers in the high Sierras are primarily fly roders but they often tuck an ultra-light spin reel in their gear for those moments when the fish are either deep or distant.

The owner of a conventional spin rod can also try for this extra potential. Mount a fly reel in place. If the rod is a fairly typical light model designed for lures in the $\frac{1}{4}$ ounce range, try a weight forward or shooting taper in 6 and 7 fly line weights and see how it works.

The spin angler who has never tried fly casting before still has one more approach that is useful when flies are obviously required. Little gadgets called spin bubbles may save the day. These are clear plastic and can be filled with water, mineral oil, etc. for casting weight. There are a couple of versions of the idea. One is a free-sliding bubble available in two sizes. The smaller one weighs $\frac{1}{4}$ ounce when filled; the larger one weighs $\frac{1}{2}$ ounce when filled. In normal use, slip the spin line through the bubble and tie a perfection loop at the end of the spin line. Above this perfection loop (and below the bubble) place a stop which can be a split shot for subsurface fly use or ust a knot of string for floating fly use. Loop a short leader onto the perfection loop you previously formed at the end of the spin line. Then tie on the appropriate fly at the end of the leader. As you make the cast, check it as the bubble nears the water to turn the leader over and extend the fly. The free-sliding bubble permits you to strike directly through to the fish with no interference from the bubble. It may not be the neatest rig in existence, but it does work and gives the spin angler the option of using flies. This extends versatility and keeps overall gear weight to a minimum.

Although we've emphasized the 6 weight outfit as generally appropriate, it is equally true that exceptions exist. Going slightly lighter or heavier may be more appropriate for your individual requirements. If you have questions, seek out expert local help from anglers and tackle shops. Also, if you want to travel light and be as flexible as possible in your approaches, try some of the experimenting outlined. Try fly lines of differing weights; try a spin reel on your fly rod; or a fly line on your spin rod. If you are a confirmed spin angler, pick up a couple of the spin bubbles and a few flies. No single method is always productive. You'll be better prepared to handle changing situations if you are aware of the various alternatives possible, even when traveling light. Certainly some of these are compromises of a sort but they work and may make the difference between taking fish and going empty-handed. As one fishing friend remarked after I'd chided him on an unorthodox, but successful, approach, "Sometimes it's better to be potent than pure."

Fly Reels

The fly reel for the backpacker is the standard single action model. As the handle makes one complete revolution, the spool also makes one complete revolution—a direct ratio. In use, the reel stores the line and backing and assists in playing the fish. The angling norm is to make the cast and immediately bring the fly line to the forefinger of the rod hand. Then all retrieves or line manipulations are done behind this rod holding hand. The handling of the line over this rod hand forefinger assures an immediate strike response and control. Any excess slack which may exist at this time is quickly taken onto the reel, and the fish is handled off the reel. A small fish may be summarily stripped in by hand, but all desirable fish require being worked off the reel. Any excess slack line always seems to find a way to tangle, causing the tippet to part and the resultant loss of the fish. Although the fly reel selected should have an adjustable drag, most experienced hands set this at the minimum setting, or just enough so the reel spool doesn't overrun when line is quickly stripped. Then the setting is never varied. The fish can be handled by rod angle counter adjustments. If additional drag is required, palm the reel. The hand provides greater response speed and sensitivity than any mechanical drag.

The usual trout reel varies from about 3 inches to some $3\frac{1}{2}$ inches in diameter, and the weight factors run from a bit under 3 ounces to over 5 ounces.

The Hardy LRH Lightweight *is one of the top of the line choices for single-action fly reel selection for any angler.*

Weight is not a functional criterion. Reel makers combine excellent strength and durability from lightweight alloys, aluminum, and other materials. The more immediate consideration is adequate capacity for the intended use, although the weight-conscious backpacker may look to the lighter end of available choices. But, by no means should weight alone be the influencing factor in making the decision. Because single action fly reels are inherently simple, some overlook quality construction features. However, any equipment malfunction or breakdown when you're far removed from an alternative is disastrous, so a quick appraisal of the apparent quality is worthwhile. For instance, the reel frame supports the spool axle and drag parts and, being subject to a great deal of vibration, it is advantageous if the number of screws in the frame construction is kept to a minimum. Further, since the axle is supported only on one side

The Cortland CG Graphite *fly reels are available in three sizes, weigh less than conventional aluminum reels, and feature adjustable drag, spool interchangeability, and easy conversion for right or left hand use.*

where it is attached to the reel frame, it must be firmly attached. The axle itself should have an adequate bearing surface to absorb the continual movement of the spool. The handle should be easy to grip, yet small and probably tapered to blend well and minimize the possibility of slack line tangling on it. A quick spool release permits access for cleaning the reel. If you are using extra spools, this feature makes for rapid and secure interchangeability. The reel foot should also be firmly secured to the frame, again so that it won't vibrate loose after a period of time.

Traditionally fly reels are seated so a right-handed caster has the reel handle on the right and changes hands while playing a fish. More and more anglers seem to be converting to left hand wind so they don't change hands. Although most reels come set up with the handle on the right, they permit easy conversion to left hand wind if the individual desires.

Have the line come to within $\frac{1}{4}$ or $\frac{3}{8}$ of an inch of the cross braces. If it doesn't, then a backing line is in order. The average trout isn't about to make a long sizzling run. However, the backing is otherwise functional in that it provides a larger arbor for the line to be wound over, minimizing any tendency for the fly line to take tight reel coils. It also permits more rapid line recovery and, of course, it is vital insurance for the occasional big trout which may decide to go places beyond the normal fly line length. Presumably many backpackers will set up a shooting taper system anyway which requires a great deal of backing if the reel is to be filled to within the $^3/_8$ of an inch of the cross braces that we recommend. Guessing at the required capacity is patently impossible. One method of working out this capacity question involves two similar capacity reels or a reel and an extra spool. Say you've got the 30 foot shooting head, the 100 feet of monofilament or level fly line and a bulk spool of 20 pound dacron or micron backing. Wind the front tip of the shooting head onto the empty reel, loop or tie the mono or level fly line, and continue winding until you come to the backing. Then loop or tie the backing and wind until the reel is almost filled (to that $^3/_8$ of an inch figure we've mentioned), and cut the backing. If you are working with a reel and an extra spool, you may now remove the spool from the reel and have someone hold it for you. Place the new empty spool in the reel and reverse wind it by tying the backing end to the reel and cranking until everything is set in a normal manner. If you have an extra reel, just reverse wind from the one to the other.

Like most choices in angling or backpacking equipment, there is a fair range of prices from which you can choose. The inflationary spirals of recent times have pushed some of the top quality reels high in price, but these products are closely machined to fine tolerances. They are durable and well made in every respect. Some of these top offerings are the fly reels from Hardy, Orvis, and Scientific Anglers. In the medium price ranges there are a larger number of choices. Careful scrutiny locates well-made, durable reels that provide trouble-free reliable service.

The Leader

The leader is critically important to the fly fisherman's success. A more or less invisible connection from the fly line to the fly, the leader must be flexible enough to permit the fly to respond to subtle current flows so the behavioral characteristics of the artificial fly appear natural and lifelike to the trout. In order for the leader to perform these multiple functions, it is tapered from a relatively large diameter butt section where it joins the fly line down through a diminishing diameter or taper graduation to the final tippet section to which the fly is attached.

Leaders are available in both knotted and knotless styles. Some specialists argue the relative merits of each but we're treading a fundamental path here, and both styles can perform admirably under most conditions as long as they are properly designed.

The usual commercial availability of tapered leaders in both styles is 7$^1/_2$ feet, 9 feet and 12 feet. On very small streams where there is apt to be a minimum of line length beyond the rod tip, and line speed may be less than normal, a short, quick turning taper is handy. The $7\frac{1}{2}$ foot lengths are usually appropriate. An average length is probably the 9 foot model. On the average-sized stream and normal casting lengths of 15 feet to 40 feet, the 9 footer carries well. If the water is very low and clear or the flies are very small, most anglers prefer the longer 12 foot models. One other relationship should be mentioned: the relationship between tippet diameter and fly size. Without a harmonious relationship here, a tiny fly may be as difficult to present properly as a much larger fly offering.

On the average, a specific diameter can support and transmit energy effectively through a range of three hook sizes. Beyond that range, chances are the tippet will require alteration to a heavier or lighter diameter for best performance. Assume you're working along with a 12 foot leader tapered to 6X with a small #20 dry in place. From a casting and presentation standpoint everything is performing well, but there are no rising fish. You decide to tie on a larger attractor type of fly such as a #12 Spider. Suddenly the smoothness is gone, the fly falls back on the leader, the leader tippet twists or it falls to lie alongside the leader rather than straightening out. What has happened is essentially this: The 6X tippet cannot support and transmit enough energy through the larger, more wind-resistant fly pattern now in place. A drastic shortening of the tippet may provide some improvement but the real answer is a larger diameter tippet that effectively supports and turns the fly properly. The following chart is a starting point for average use:

tippet size	fly size	tippet size	fly size
0X (.011)	2 to 1/0	5X (.006)	14,16,18
1X (.010)	4,6,8	6X (.005)	16-22
2X (.009)	6,8,10	7X (.004)	18-28
3X (.008)	10,12,14	8X (.003)	20-28
4X (.007)	12,14,16		

Related to this discussion is monofilament "memory" or its tendency to retain tight packaging coils. These should be removed before starting to fish. Most limp materials can be straightened by hand. Pull to stretch them somewhat, then gradually release the tension. Additionally there are commercial aids, leader conditioners of leather or rubber. The tops of your rubber waders are handy for this. If the heavier butt portions haven't straightened satisfactorily by hand, the conditioners are useful. Be sure not to rub too vigorously. Frictional heat is generated and too much heat may damage the molecular structure of the monofilament. The monofilament has a specific gravity somewhat in excess of water. In theory it will sink by itself. However, the tendency is for it to remain buoyed up by normal surface tension. There are a number of commercial leader sinks which some anglers regularly use. Others question or discount the importance of a leader tippet floating or sinking in normal dry fly use and ignore the question entirely. Their continued successes tend to indicate that in most instances a natural, drag free and lifelike behavior of the artificial fly which is achieved through tippet length and flexibility is a more important consideration than whether the tippet floats or sinks. Still, there may be specific instances when a portion of the tippet should be sunk. Lacking a commercial preparation use mud, silt, or aquatic vegetation to "treat" the section. If you want to be sure the leader will float while fishing emergent or floating mayfly nymphs, midge pupae or caddis pupae, treat the leader with any of the silicone based preparations such as *Mucilin* or *Gink*.

Although the 7½, 9 and 12 footers are the commercial norm, there are occasions when longer or shorter leaders can be used. Several pond and lake specialists working with floating lines are going to very long knotted tapers of 20 feet or more. Conversely, anglers using sinking lines have found that deep-lying fish are not leader shy. To counteract the natural tendency for the leader to sink very slowly, more slowly than their sinking fly lines, they compensate by shortening their leaders, which may run from about 2 feet to 6 feet in length. These can be as simple as a single strand of monofilament or no more than three pieces of monofilament of different diameters knotted together. The level at which a fly works is vital. These extra short leaders are very effective. From a standpoint of simplicity, there is one more system that is gaining in popularity with some anglers. It consists of making a permanent loop in the end of the leader and looping the desired tippet to it in a loop to loop connection. The looped tippets are prepared beforehand at home and quickly added on the stream. In fact, if you have an idea of what fly you'll want to use as dusk settles, you can prepare totally in advance by knotting on the fly choice to the other end of the looped tippet and minimize the struggles as dusk settles and the activity starts.

The backpacker's needs are often variable with the water types he encounters, so it's probably best to acquire a basic set of tapers in the 7½, 9 and 12 foot lengths as a starting point. Add a few spools of tippet material in the required size ranges, and you'll be able to adjust for whatever conditions are encountered.

Tackle Selection

As separate activities, both backpacking and fishing are potentially gadget-laden endeavors. When they're combined the situation is even more complex. A careful appraisal of an item's usefulness-to-weight ratio is essential for trips of any length.

In addition to the specifics of tackle item selection is the question of rod case transport. I've seen some backpackers carry the rod case in hand, using it as a walking staff of sorts. However, if both hands are needed to negotiate a tough stretch of terrain, this is a real nuisance. Kelty used to (and may still) offer a better answer in an inexpensive little item they called a fish pole sock. Essentially it looks like a tube sock, 1¾ inches in diameter and 6 inches long with a draw string at the top. A rod case of any length can be enclosed. The idea is to tie it to the packframe side member just above a cross bar and let the sock support the weight of the rod. The upper part of the rod case can be secured parallel to the frame side member with a sturdy elastic band, or perhaps better yet, it can be taped in place. As an alternative to the fish pole sock, I've used an old reel bag in the same way, tying it to the frame and taping the upper part of the rod case in place. Something like this can easily be made up at home, and is much easier than trying to carry a rod case in hand.

If the destination is a pond or lake, I add the weight of either a float tube (belly boat) or an inflatable pack raft. There are few things more frustrating than walking several miles to a backcountry pond and finding all the fish working out of reach. The weight and space of either accessory is worthwhile.

Tony Atwill takes to the water with an inflatable pack raft. Just under 5 lbs. in total weight, the use of such a raft opens up new opportunities for the backpacking angler.

I've had both items for several years and they've always performed admirably. In addition to my pack raft's normal use of moving me from here to there on the water, it's seen some service as a wilderness bathtub, weather shelter, and even a boat bed. I carry some lightweight rope which can be marked heavily at measured intervals with a permanent pen marker, or knotted at intervals to help determine depth. A rock can be tied to the end of the rope to help as a depth probe and anchor of sorts as well. Despite a lot of hard use the raft has stood up extremely well, but I've been concerned about future replacement possibilities, as my American Safety raft has been discontinued. Fortunately Del Canty has come along with an alternative and the only lightweight pack raft that I'm currently aware of. Del is a very skilled specialist who has been taking giant trout for years from float tubes and to a lesser extent from pack rafts. The basic specifications of his pack raft read just about the same as my old American Safety standby, and the use of such a lightweight, portable, and durable pack raft can do wonders for the angling results in many areas.

When I don't take the pack raft, it is the belly boat that goes along. There are "plastic fins" on the market that help propel you around in the float tube, but I prefer swim fins. These can be carried in the pack or lashed outside the pack when walking.

For backcountry river work when wading is required, I use the new Royal Red Ball *Flyweight* stocking foot waders and their felt-soled wading shoes. The waders only weigh only about 12 ounces and are amazingly tough and durable. These have filled a real need for the backcountry angler, and are proving equally popular for normal day to day angling as well.

Beyond these specialized items, the tackle selection is up to the individual. For most trips, not much gear has to be taken. Most tackle will probably all fit in a side pocket of the pack. Generally a fishing vest isn't needed. If one is deemed necessary, the two lightest weight possibilities I'm aware of are the *Warm Weather Tac-L-Pak* from Orvis and the *Furnace Creek Vest* from Tim Boyle at Columbia Sportswear in Portland, Oregon. Each is essentially a bunch of holes held together by nylon with ample pocket capacity for the needs of any packer-angler. Some hikers carry their gear in a small belt bag or fanny pack. Also, an inexpensive day bag may be a handy accessory for splinter day travels out of an established camp site. Normally I just head out with the Orvis *Fishing Shirt*. It's comfortable on the trail, and the large pockets hold all the flies and small accessories I'll need. If more pockets are needed, they can be added at home with a modicum of sewing ability. These added, extra pockets can then be sized and located to suit individual requirements.

A few items may be considered more or less standard for both backpacking and backcountry fishing: a knife, rain jacket, insect repellent, a hat, and polarized sunglasses. The hat and sunglasses are also safety precautions on windy days when working from the pack raft or belly boat—just in case an errant cast swings in too close to you.

Specifically—do you have, want or need:

pack raft or float tube
lightweight stocking foot waders and wading shoes

fly rod, spin rod or combination fly-spin rod appropriate to destination water
types and requirements
fly reel with extra spool and line or fly reel with a variety of shooting tapers
leaders and extra tippet materials
plastic or aluminum fly boxes and desired fly types and sizes
spin reel with extra spool of heavier or lighter line
tape—to secure a spin reel to a fly rod cork grip for special purpose
double duty use of the fly rod as a spin rod accommodation
spin bubble—for using flies on a spin rod if desired
ball bearing snap swivels
lure box with variety of spin lures
fishing shirt or alternative—vest, belt bag, fanny pack and light day bag
folding net—i.e., North Fork *pocket net or* Insta-Net *by Handy Pak*
Flex-Light or similar small, convenient alternative
weights—split shot, twist-on lead, lead sleeves or alternatives
strike indicator—for subsurface fly work when using floating line methods
scissor pliers, folding scissors, or angler's clipper

leader conditioner	*rain jacket*
leader sink	*knife*
line cleaner/dressing	*hat*
fly floatant	*polaroids*
stream thermometer	*insect repellent*

hook hone—to touch up dulled hooks
Dry-Ur-Fly *absorbent powder to restore soaked and matted flies*
permanent pen markers to alter colors of flies as needed
surgical forceps as hook disgorger
Perhaps a bit more specialized—*aquarium net for picking insects off the water*
to determine size, color, etc.; insect collecting vials; stomach pump; magni-
fying glass; portable fly tying gear; notebook and pencil; Arcticreel; *and*
whistle for emergency use.

Don't be concerned about the length or complexity of these listings. They serve as an overview of a range of possibilities. The individual should select or modify to suit his or her own needs. Here, for instance, is the go-light approach of one friend for small to medium-sized back country streams in the Northeast. He ties a series of dries in two styles and three sizes. The styles are parachute and a Wingless Hackle pattern that comes out looking like a spider; the sizes are 12, 16 and 20. They're made up in only one light color. He explains that the parachute is low floating, invariably lands upright on the water, and is stable in any water type from slow to fast. The Wingless Hackle patterns have a slightly oversized hackle spread (a #16 would have a normal-sized #14 hackle) to provide a contrasting approach of a higher riding, sparser silhouette. At streamside he alters both types with permanent pen markers to suit the color requirements of the moment. For evening spinner falls he scissors the hackled patterns top and bottom for a reasonable shape approximation. He's adding

Only about 12 ounces, the Royal Red Ball stocking foot wader system is ideal for the backcountry angler and is proving equally popular for normal day to day angling.

another "down wing" series of flies for this season to suggest caddis and stonefly activity.

Some of these flies will be made up on 2X and 3X long shank hooks. When appropriately colored at streamside with pen markers, he figures they will be close enough for cricket and grasshopper activity as well. He does carry a few distinctive shapes, such as ants and beetles, which are otherwise difficult to obtain by alteration. A standard, all purpose nymph like the Gold Ribbed Hare's Ear is tied on standard shank lengths as well as longer shanks. A few are also made up on dry fly hooks for emergent or floating nymph activity. These are also fine tuned as needed with permanent pen markers. For wet flies he relies on a few standards such as a dark Wooly Worm, Picket Pin, Breadcrust, and Brown Hackle Peacock. They supplement his bait fish imitations of Muddler, Grey Ghost, Black Nose Dace and White Marabou.

Some fly floatant, twist-on leads, folding scissors, spare leaders, and tippet material make up the other basic items. If a specific fly is expected to be of particular importance (such as the mid to late season "Trico") he'll make up specific imitations. But overall his frame of mind is to get as much mileage out of a minimum amount of gear as possible. He succeeds surprisingly well. Adding to this success is his experience and careful observation. He pays a great deal of attention to approaching working fish and takes time to maneuver around to a good position or angle from which to deliver his casts accurately and neatly. These down-to-earth requirements are important factors of angling consistency.

Lure Selection

A quick visit to the nearest, well-stocked tackle shop or an evening spent reading through a few angling catalogs reveals a bewildering array of available spin lures. At the other extreme there are some experienced hands who depend wholly on a specific lure or type of lure. If that singular approach fails them, the fish simply aren't hitting. Nestled somewhere between these extremes there is a functional, common sense starting point. There is a long way between tackle shops in the backcountry, so versatility is the ultimate goal.

The basic types of lures for the spin fisherman are spinners, spoons, jigs, and plugs. A starting selection should be made within this framework.

SPINNERS: The little mountain stream sparkled invitingly in the midsummer sun as we shed our packs and took a break from our sweaty hike. As we sat, sipping the cool water, an angler rounded the downstream bend. We watched as he flipped a little lure about twenty-five feet upstream into a shallow run. He angled the rod far to his right and began retrieving, guiding the lure close to the shadowy side of a large boulder. A chunky little rainbow knifed out to intercept the swim and was soon landed.

A few moments later the angler joined us and noted that this was his fourth fish of the morning. A look at the stream and you'd have thought there wasn't a trout in it. The droughty conditions revealed every pebble, yet tucked away in pools wherever there was a semblance of cover were spunky little trout. The visiting angler had chosen the right weapons for these conditions: a short five foot rod, ultra-light real spooled with two pound mono and a tiny $\frac{1}{16}$th ounce spinner. This stream is typical of many small, mountainous waters in mid-summer: barely moist in the shallows, then dropping off into little runs and pools a foot or so deep.

Conventional $\frac{1}{4}$ ounce spinners or spoons would have been almost impossible to manipulate in the skinny water, their weight demanding a hastier retrieve else they sink artlessly to the bottom. The little lightweight spinner could twinkle along slowly and made all the difference. The angler had also handled the little spinner correctly, first estimating where the fish might lie and casting far enough above the suspected hideaway so he wouldn't alarm the fish. This permitted him to get the lure under control, establish a fishable depth, and steer the lure close to cover. These are sound tactics regardless of the method employed.

In shallow waters spinners are often easier to handle than wobbling spoons, for the revolving blade offers increased resistance, permitting a slow, snag-free retrieve. If choosing between two spinners of equal weight but different blade size, the general rule is that the larger of the two blades offers increased resistance. This allows a slower retrieve which is often better in shallow sections, slow-water sections, and in lakes when fish are cruising near the surface. A narrow-bladed spinner requires more water pressure. Therefore, it fishes deeper and handles better in quick stream runs. Both types have their obvious uses and advantages.

Occasionally the configuration of the stream is such that a downstream cast is needed. If this is the case, the spinners offer excellent lure control. They can be worked back at varying speeds or even held steady. In spite of the sometime advantage in downstream directions, the general rule is to take advantage of the trout's into-the-current posture and work upstream. Closer approaches, enhanced accuracy, and lure control are some of the upstream directed advantages. Tactically, the thinking is the same, whether on an upstream or downstream path. Aim the cast beyond the anticipated lie of the fish and steer the lure to work in close to the suspected hotspot. Swim the lure to the fish at an effective level rather than dropping it in on his head. Attract the fish, don't alarm it.

In large streams thorough water coverage is the prerequisite approach. Try casts angled upstream and just slightly across the current, bringing the lure back at about the same speed as the existing current. Casting cycles should always be progressive in nature, starting close and extending outward in successive casts. When the upstream areas within easy reach are covered, try casting across and just slightly upstream and allow the lure to work around in semicircular sweeps. Enlarge on this concept with successive casts progres-

103

sively covering a bit more water. When all the reachable water has been thoroughly covered, move and start again with the progressive short, medium, long casting coverages. You should, of course, always be alert for any singular fish holding possibilities which may exist along current edges: drop offs from shallow to deeper waters, along fallen logs, by bouldery obstructions, near undercut banks, and the like.

In the little streams the $\frac{1}{16}$th ounce spinners are about ideal and there would be a bit of leeway for both slightly lighter and slightly heavier lures. In larger rivers the lures can be scaled up and the 3/16th to $\frac{1}{4}$ ounce sizes are apt to be more suitable.

A basic selection of spinners should include a variety of finishes or color combinations. Try to select something with dull or dark tones, then something with medium tones, and finally choose something with light or bright tones. This enables you to suit a lure to specific water clarity conditions.

SPOONS: Spoons are among the most popular of the various spin lures for the fundamental reason that they are very effective. Their selection can be related in part to water conditions, depths to be fished, and perhaps even the time of year. Our twin activities of backpacking and angling are primarily three-season sports. Early in the season, when the ice has recently left the ponds and lakes, the water temperature is about the same from top to bottom. Trout tend to work the shallow waters actively at this time. In many areas, such as the northeastern lakes, there may be smelt runs into various tributary streams. We can expect trout and landlocked salmon to forage aggressively through such schooling fish. A wobbling spoon that will fish high in the water is an excellent choice. When selecting between two spoons of equal weight but different blade size, we can expect the larger blade to sink more slowly and handle higher in the water. This characteristic is the ideal for our early season pond and lake activity, and perhaps again late in the fall when cooler waters prevail and the trout are prowling the shallows with some consistency.

The spoons with the smaller surface area for equal weight do cast more easily against strong winds, tend to work deeper, and sink more rapidly. These characteristics are suited to summer conditions when the depths of various ponds and lakes must be plumbed. Also, in the large, swift streams, the denser spoons are ideal.

The standard large stream starting point is to angle the cast up and somewhat across stream, bringing the wobbler back at about the same speed as the current flow and working it deep. Then you may work into a sweeping semicircular coverage. Cast across stream and just slightly upriver, let the wobbler flutter down and angle around. Enlarge on this concept with slightly larger, progressive, casting arcs.

In the small intimate waters, stick to lightweight spoons around the $\frac{1}{16}$th ounce size. For the larger rivers the one quarter ounce size is again the standard starting point.

There are several lure finishes: gold, brass, copper, silver, black, pearl or abalone and, of course, all the color combinations from red and white through the current craze for natural "fish scale" types. As a starting point I believe it's safest to consider overall tonal values and pick something dull or dark, then a medium tonal value, and finally something light or bright. A final check with a tackle dealer in the general area of your trip can suggest any specific local favorites.

PLUGS: Although they are usually associated with heavier bait casting gear and fish other than trout, there are enough mini-plugs available today to demand the attention of the well-rounded spin tackle fan.

Plugs are essentially best suited to the larger streams and ponds. If your backcountry parameters will include these water types, a few plugs are a worthwhile addition to your kit. One advantage of the backpacking angler is that he can set up camp near a stream or pond and not worry about being back for some arbitrary deadline. Large brown trout are notorious night feeders through much of the season, and in the heat of midsummer we can expect an activity burst near dawn. The small surface disturbing plugs provide exceptional results under such conditions. They should be fished very slowly, gurgling and pausing in suggestion of wounded or crippled prey. The various shallow, running and small-jointed plugs also do well under these conditions. On the large streams pay particular attention to the shallow runs ahead of the main pools, then work slowly through the pool to the tailing shallows. Large brown trout do much foraging after dark and they can often be found in surprisingly shallow water seeking small crayfish, minnows and other food forms.

The spring, as streams begin to clear but are still running a bit too cold for good insect activity, is another time when plug-handling anglers score well on large rainbows and browns. During the day they often take up feeding stations beneath and beside fairly heavy main current tongues. The minnow-suggestive plugs do a good job. One angling acquaintance swears by the smaller Rapalas and countdown Rapalas for this time period. His catches are impressive.

JIGS: Of all the lures common to the average spin angler's arsenal the jigs are the most overlooked, yet, they have uncommon significance by providing an approach impossible to duplicate with spinners, spoons or plugs. On the broad assumption that these other lures suggestively resemble baitfish and have inherently different action in the water, the common bond between them is that they are usually kept on the move. I know they can take fish when held stationary downstream but most strikes do occur when they are on the move.

Now, consider the jig. It has been used most often in a vertical path. That is, it may be cast from a boat. When it hits bottom it is moved up and down, eventually brought back to the surface and recast. Experienced bonefishermen on southern flats have been using jigs in essentially a horizontal travel with great success. The jig can also be inhaled while sitting stationary. Every trout stream has deep holes or undercut banks where large trout dominate. When the fish are not out in a feeding posture, a lure must travel deep to be seen by these cave dwellers. Deep running wobblers and plugs sometimes draw these fish out, but many of these lazy, domineering fish are reluctant to swing out to a rapidly moving lure. The bottom knocking jig is an approach of singular value. It can be cast, allowed to sink to the bottom and then moved slowly or brought along in bouncing hippity-hopping motions. This is because of the weight distribution of the jig, with its hook at the top and its nose-first sinking action. The jigs may resemble some sculpin, large nymphs, or crayfish. In this regard I'm reminded of a call a few years ago from one of the nation's leading anglers, discussing the possibility of a fall trip to Montana. During the conversation we somehow got on the subject of unusual applications of various flies and lures. He mentioned that the Wiggle Jig, a bonefish lure, had long been a secret weapon for large trout. He was convinced that the stop and go manipulations possible with the Wiggle Jig suggested a small crayfish.

The initial presentations are up and across stream, allowing the jig to work deep and pumping the rod tip to slowly bounce the jig along in erratic, tantalizing hippity-hops. In large streams the jig can work out in a cross-stream move; then let it swing around to a position directly below you. Pump the rod and lower the rod tip to allow the lure to settle on the bottom. Tease it along in a pause and pull motion. Pay particular attention to the open sides of log jams, undercut banks and other deep cover that may harbor a good fish.

The jigs are also effective in ponds and lakes. They work deep in weed bed channels, along drop off edges and other potential spots. At night try the shallows when the large fish move in close under the cover of darkness.

For the average small streams the $\frac{1}{16}$th ounce size is again a good starting point, scaling upwards for the larger, deeper rivers. The first few color choices might be green, brown, and black.

A final consideration that is most important with the single-hooked jigs is to keep them sharp. They are the one lure that may be scooped off the bottom when sitting stationary, so penetration is essential.

9.

REGIONAL RECOMMENDATIONS

Tips from the Local Experts

Any trout producing area of the country offers great potential for the opportunistic, free-to-go-anywhere angler willing to investigate. Trips can be tailered to seasonal availability and angling interest. Small backcountry streams or ponds, or large rivers or high altitude lakes are all within the scope of the hiker. With some judicious planning there may be the further bonus of angling for very large trout. The consistent taking of large fish is a specialty. It is sound, practical angling requiring skill, patience, and knowledge. Perhaps there's no one quite so qualified to discuss taking large trout consistently as Del Canty. He's devoted years of study and practical application to the development of a "system." In addition to his angling skills, Del is a thoroughly experienced backpacker. He has a small booklet (published by Del Canty's Lunker Hunter Systems, Inc., Leadville, Colorado) highlighting his methods. With his permission we've culled a few observations. For large lakes and floatable rivers he uses either the float tube or the backpacker boat, although his preference is the float tube. With this qualification in mind, here is a part of his comment on basic lake fishing methods.

From Del Canty

"The best method is to parallel the shoreline and make casts toward the bank. I usually start out in the afternoon and just wander along, casting every few feet. I don't try to cast very far because it becomes very tiring. However, if I see the movement of what I think is a large fish, I'll make a long cast to him while

I think I know where he is. It doesn't pay to wait 'til you get to the fish before casting. Blind casts are not nearly as effective as casting at a target. Early in the evening, I place my line of travel in about 20 feet of water. This way I can usually reach the 10 foot level, and if I cast out, the 30 foot level. On dark days it is better to be on a line of travel over about 10 or 12 feet of water and to cast into about 5 or 6 feet of water. On bright days you may want to be over the 30 foot level so you can reach the 20 and 40 foot depths. Lakes vary as to drop-off depths, so adjust accordingly. One rule of thumb is to use dark flies on light days, and light flies on dark days. In the daytime I usually use a sinking line and at night I use a floating line and a floating or nearly floating fly. I also move into shallower water at night."

About fishing rivers—*"Large rivers are fished differently from small. This deals with rivers that are floatable. I usually have all my gear aboard either the Boat or Float and watch ahead for spots where I can either come ashore or hold my position by paddling. Occasionally I find places where I can anchor and hit good water.*

You must learn what is prime water and what is not. Some of the best spots are: at the base of a riffle where fast waters enter slow water; where a coarse gravel bar with open gravel exists to provide good cover for insect brood stock; watch for the deep hole with boulders to provide cover; pocket water with scattered large boulders is also good; big logs will also provide cover; undercut banks are excellent; log jams are also very good; weed beds exist in some slow rivers and provide good cover. Always remember that both the fish and their food require cover. Train yourself to look for cover and your fishing will drastically improve.

A floating line is proper where the river is not deep. The sinking line is proper where deep holes are fished or in large deep rivers. Casting to your spots is a good basic technique and works well in most cases. This means casting at angles upstream and down. Sometimes feeding a long line into cover from above will take the wise old fish, so keep it in mind. The real trick is to get yourself into the right position for presentation without making the fish aware of your presence.

Small rivers where you can or must wade are best fished with a long nymphing rod and the short line method. Two techniques work well. You can either wade up the stream or stay out of the stream and hit prime spots. In either case, you do not actually cast. Your line is almost always straight down from the rod tip so you can effectively bump your nymph along the bottom lifting it about three inches off the bottom for each bump. When a fish touches your nymph you know it right away.

On all rivers, large and small, a study of the available food will tell you what flies and lures to use. Turn over rocks, gather vegetation to see what is hiding there. Always remember, though, the Lunker will be found feeding on large enough fare to sustain his weight."

There is, of course, considerably more in the Del Canty booklet, but even this

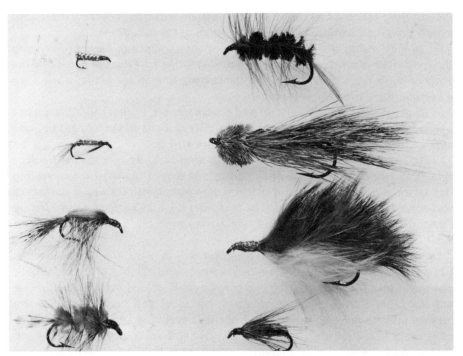

Del Canty's Fly Recommendations for Wind River area, Bridger Wilderness:

1. *Copepod*
2. *Grey Nymph*
3. *Grizzly Shrimp*
4. *Wooly Worm—orange body*
5. *Wooly Worm—fluorescent hackle*
6. *Badger Muddler*
7. *Rabbit Minnow*
8. *Moth*

cursory overview helps to indicate the thought process, attention to detail, and purposeful curiosity of the specialist. These are qualities which all anglers are advised to cultivate.

In addition to these qualities, some local knowledge is always advantageous. A number of fine anglers have very kindly offered basic recommendations for regions with which they are particularly familiar.

MARYLAND THROUGH NORTH CAROLINA MOUNTAINS

From Lefty Kreh

Tackle needed for the streams in the mountains of Maryland south through western North Carolina is fortunately simple.

So far as ultra-light spinning gear is concerned, about all you require is a reel carrying 4 pound test line. Two lures will do the trick in every stream, and actually one will work in 90 percent or more of the situations.

I'd suggest using a #0 gold Mepps spinner. It does not have to have any squirrel tail or other adornments. In small streams I let it wash down into the heads of pools from above, allowing the current to spin the blade, while I try to keep the lure near the bottom.

In larger pools I toss the lure up and across stream, so that the blade doesn't turn too fast when you bring it back. Silver Mepps will do the job, but in these clear waters the gold finish seems to be more effective.

I also carry the two-inch gold Rapala floating lure. Be sure it's the floating style. You can fish this by throwing down and across the stream and reeling back in an erratic manner, and you can also toss it into the upper portion of a calm pool and then bring it back by twitching it on the surface, rarely letting it go under. This represents a live, struggling minnow, which few trout can resist.

As for flies, a basic and simple selection will do here, too. If you use the Adams in sizes 12, 16, and 18 (smaller flies are more effective after mid-June), then you'll take fish that are rising to gray or dark-colored insects. And, if you cast the Light Cahill in the same sizes, the trout will respond if they are working over lighter-colored insects. Generally speaking, the Adams will work better early in the season, and the Cahill after mid-June. Along about the end of May there are hatches in incredible numbers of light green inchworms. At this time an imitation is deadly.

As for wet flies, the Lead Wing Coachman and the Hare's Ear are two flies local trouters won't be without.

For nymphs, Poul Jorgensen's light brown, medium and dark brown nymphs, which are tied from fur and really resemble all nymphs, but none in particular are deadly. Most nymphs should be no larger than size 10, and many times those tied on 14 and 16 hooks are better.

The White and Black Marabou are standard early spring streamers. Later, say by June, the smaller imitative streamers, such as the Black Nose Dace and the Spruce Fly are effective. In a summary sentence—you don't need a lot of lure or flies, just a wise selection.

ADIRONDACKS

From Lionel Atwill

DRY FLIES

Ausable Wulff
Henryville Special
Adams
Blue Wing Olive
Grey Fox

WET FLIES

Royal Coachman
Montreal
March Brown

SPINNING LURES

Red/White Daredevle
Yellow Jig
Mepps Black Fury
Panther Martin

NYMPHS

Green Drake
Zug Bug
Hare's Ear
Dark Stonefly

STREAMERS

Muddler Minnow
Black Matuka
Grey Ghost

VERMONT

From John Merwin

DRY FLIES: #14 Adams, #20 Black Midge, #14 Woodchuck Caddis
WET FLIES: #14 Gold-Ribbed Hare's Ear, #14 Royal Coachman, #14 Black Ant
NYMPHS: #14 Tan Caddis Pupa, #14 Hendrickson, #8 Hexagenia Wiggle-Nymph
STREAMERS: #6 Muddler, #6 Mickey Finn, #6 Badger Matuka
SPINNING LURES:

3" Floating Rapala, silver with black back
Silver or Gold Flatfish; any of so-called fly-rod sizes
Mepps spinner, $1/8$-oz., silver or gold
Pheobe Spoon, $1/8$-oz., gold

NEW HAMPSHIRE

From Dick Surette

SPRING

April—May

Streamers		Wet Flies	
Mickey Finn	*6—10*	*Black Gnat*	*10—12*
Grey Ghost	*6—10*	*Blue Dun*	*10—12*
Nine Three	*6—10*	*Brown Hackle*	*10—12*
Supervisor	*6—10*	*Hornberg*	*6—10*
Black Ghost	*6—10*	*Montreal*	*10—12*

Dry Flies		Nymphs	
Black Gnat	*12—14*	*Black Nymph*	*12—12*
Black Midge	*20—28*	*Montana*	*6—10*
Quill Gordon	*12—14*	*Black Sparrow*	*8—12*
Royal Wulff	*10—12*	*Golden Stonefly*	*6*

EARLY SUMMER

June 1—July 15

Streamers		Wet Flies	
Grey Ghost	*8—10*	*Quill Gordon*	*10—12*
Matuka	*8—12*	*Hare's Ear*	*10—12*
Harris Special	*6—10*	*Dk. Hendrikson*	*10—12*
Golden Demon	*6—10*	*Hornberg*	*10—14*
Black Ghost	*6—10*	*Muddler*	*8—12*

Dry Flies		Nymphs	
Adams	*12—14*	*Zug Bug*	*10—12*
Red Quill	*12—14*	*Hare's Ear*	*8—14*
Grey Fox Variant	*12—16*	*Olive Green Caddis*	*10—12*
Henryville Special	*12—16*	*March Brown*	*12—14*
Cream Caddis	*12—14*	*Brown Nymph*	*12—16*
Hendrikson	*12—16*		

LATE SUMMER

July 15—Sept. 1

Streamers		Wet Flies	
Black Nose Dace	8—12	Professor	10—12
Llama	8—12	Lt. Cahill	10—12
Maynard Marvel	8—12	Hornberg	12—16
Little Brook Trout	6—10	Muddler	12—14
Ballou Special	6—10	Gray Hackle	10—12

Dry Flies		Nymphs	
Grasshopper	10—14	Atherton Light	14
Spiders	14	Hare's Ear	12—16
Adams	14—18	Caddis Pupa	10—12
Ginger Bivisible	12—14	Midge Pupa	18—20
Blue Wing Olive	16—18		
Cream Midge	20		
Black Beetle	18		

FALL

Sept. 1—Oct. 15

Streamers		Wet Flies	
Dk. Edson Tiger	6—14	Muddler	6—10
Lt. Edson Toger	6—14	Hornberg	6—10
Royal Coachman	8—12	Royal Coachman	10—12
Warden's Worry	6—10	Black Gnat	14—16
Mickey Finn	10—12	Gray Hackle	10—12

Dry Flies		Nymphs	
Grasshopper	8—12	Casual Dress	8
Royal Wulff	10—12	Hare's Ear	8—12
Black Ant	14—20	Crayfish	6—10
Bucktail Caddis	8—12	Olive Nymph	12—16
Blue Dun Midge	20		

MAINE

From Bob Leeman

When I'm wading or canoeing the central and eastern regions of Maine for Brook Trout, I'm sure to include in my flybox the following selections of flies:

Muddler minnows in sizes ranging from #12 to #8. The muddlers work especially well if there's a slight rise in water, or if it's the least bit turgid.

Grasshoppers: preferably yellow, but some orange. The size #8 hoppers seem to lure the biggest trout to strike.

Buckbugs in sizes 10 and 12. Here's a relatively new fly to us from Canadian waters. I don't really know what the Brookies think it is, but they're intent on destroying it. And, they'll take it fished both wet and dry.

Cahills #12 and #14 in both light and dark shades and Slim Jims in the same sizes are my preferred dry flies.

Parmacheene Belle #14 dries are best on a real bright day on crystalline waters.

Hornbergs and Humpys in size 10 are excellent for both Brookies and Brown Trout. Slightly larger sizes are good for landlocked salmon while casting rivers that have them. The Browns seem to have a passion for yellow colors, so I carry some Yellow Hornbergs especially for them.

I've taken some heavy Landlocked Salmon and trout too, on #12 Picket Pins that come under the category of nymph-wet type flies.

The Green Caddis Latex nymph is always in my flybox during the early part of the season. A Hare's Ear nymph is good, too. Both are weighted.

Professors and Royal Coachmans in sizes #10 and #12 are preferred wet fly patterns. Mosquitoes in small sizes tied real sparse in both wet and dry patterns will often produce when all else fails with finicky trout.

My best casting streamer fly patterns in bigger waters include: Grey Ghost, Pink Lady, Maribou Muddler, and Red and White Bucktail. Best sizes in these are #8 and #10. I try not to forget a Barnes Special for any interested Browns.

There's also the exception to the basic rules. For those occasions which fishermen cannot explain, I always include (and often try) a big #8 White Wulff dryfly and a #8 brown and orange stonefly dryfly.

During late season, low-water September fishing, sizes #18 to #24 Midge dryflies have often saved the day for action. Brown, Black, and Blue Dun patterns are best.

When my ultra-light spinning outfit goes along for both river and pond casting, I make sure I have the following lures with me: Dardevle Midgets in red and white and yellow five-of-diamonds, Al's Goldfish in gold, and a few small, assorted Mepps Spinners in both silver and gold. With this arsenal, I consider myself well prepared. And, everything is light, compact, and easily portaged.

MIDWEST

From Dick Pobst

For the Great Lakes area, we have several different types of fishing to consider. All are with flies and all are in rivers or streams.

In spring we start with the steelhead, usually in late March or early April. Typical fly selections include the Spring Nymph, as the most popular, and some of the western patterns such as Skunk, Umpqua, and Skykomish, all on size 4 hooks. However, we have recently found that the steelhead are highly selective to the stonefly nymphs that are active in the water; so now my first choices are a large black stonefly nymph, size 2, and the early black, size 8. Last spring we found that on some days we would get strikes on more than half our casts with the stoneflies.

The streamer fisherman would usually be well served with a selection of Muddlers, Matukas, and Black-Nosed Daces.

After trout opening day, the last Saturday in April, the early trout fisherman wants to pay special attention to the Midwestern super-hatch chart from Selective Trout. He should have: Hendricksons, size 14; Sulfur Duns, #16; Blue-Winged Olives, #18. In addition, there is a very prolific little Black Caddis, size 16. The Gray Drake, #12, is important on some rivers.

For the mid-season, the major hatches are the Brown Drake, #10, and the giant Michigan Mayfly, #6, which hatches after dark. Besides those, it is good to have some #14 light Cahills and #14 and #16 Adams. In case you happen to run into an important caddis hatch, we'd suggest #18 Henryvilles and #16 Kings River patterns. This season is from about the first of June to the 10th of July.

For the late trout season, you have: Slate-winged Olives, size 14; White-Winged Blacks, #26; and tiny Blue-Winged Olives, #24. It is also important to have some terrestrials, such as hoppers and ants. Night fisherman use big flies, such as mouse and frog patterns that are used on bass, or big streamers.

Sometime in September, the Chinook and Coho Salmon start to move into the rivers. At first they can be taken by fishing big streamers deep in the heads of pools at dusk. By big streamers I mean ones with an overall length of 4 to 6 inches. However, our rivers are short, and once the spawning urge takes hold, the fish move directly from the lake to the spawning redds. We then fish to spotted fish, concentrating on the big dominant males, which run from 25 to 40 pounds, and are very tough. For those we use two-egg sperm flies and salmon muddlers, as well as the steelhead flies, usually on #4 hooks.

For spinning, the most popular lures are Mepps spinners fished upstream on ultralight tackle, and there are some very creative fishermen with Rapalas. Quite a few spin with nymphs and split shot.

The Keel Flies that are most popular are the Muddler and Black-Nosed Dace for fishing some of the loggy, brushy streams (streamer flies).

The Keel Dry flies have gained greatest acceptance in the U.S. for fishing the giant mayfly hatch, since it is so easy to get hung up when fishing after dark. Interestingly, the Keel dries have made major impact on the chalk streams of England, due to the interest of Dermot Wilson. John Goddard plans to feature them in a forthcoming book on chalk stream fishing. The reason is that they ride with the hook out of the water, and have the natural curved body of the mayfly.

The other Keel flies that have done very well are the floating bass bugs, called Miracle Bugs by Al McClane, and the saltwater patterns.

COLORADO

From Charlie Loughridge

DRIES—(in the high country). #16—18 Royal Wulff, #18—20 Mosquito, #18—20 Black Gnat, #18—20 Light Cahill, #16—18 Grey Parachute (these with a very short deer hair tail, white kip tail wing and brown hackle), #8—10 Grasshoppers, #12—16 Caddis, such as elk hair caddis.

WET—Black Wooly Worms #8—10 (without tinsel ribbing, use either brown or grizzly hackle).

Other General Recommendations for Colorado Waters: Dry—Adams in #14 and smaller, #12 Royal Wulff and smaller, #20 and 22 Grey Herl Midges. Wets: Grey Hackle Yellow #12, #12 Cowdung. Nymphs: #12—16 weighted, Gold Ribbed Hare's Ear, Muskrat, Renegade and dark stoneflies in #10 through 16. For general spinning, the smaller sizes Mepps spinners in both gold and silver work well.

WYOMING

From Del Canty

My favorite flies for Wind River Area, Bridger Wilderness:

Copepod—for the lakes that contain Goldens and other waters that are ideal habitat for Goldens. This means those lakes above 9,500 ft. that have large populations of Copepods. The real thing is about $1/_{32}$ to $1/_{16}$ of an inch long, occasionally up to $1/_8$ inch. The fly is obviously oversize, but it works so don't *tell the fish, please.*

Grey Nymph—Represents the Burrowing May, several Caddis and the Grey Midges. It's a good all-around nymph and easy to tie.

Grizzly Shrimp—Good wherever Gammarus Scuds exist. That will be wherever the fish are exceptionally plump. The fly is oversize, but again, don't tell the fish!

Wooly Worm—Orange Body is for spawning fish.

Wooly Worm—Fluorescent hackle for murky water. Fished deep and down the bank, best from float or boat.

Badger Muddler—Wherever minnows exist.

Rabbit Minnow—Wherever minnows exist.

Moth—For moths, evening fishing with floating line.

When backpacking, I use the Fishing Float, Bivouac Bag Inflator, *light swim fins, lightweight waders and* Air Pillow *whenever the per day distance is less than 8 miles. The total weight of this outfit is heavier and also limits me to only about a 5 days' supply of food. I don't like my pack to go over 40 pounds.*

If I'm on a long trail, (8 to 20 miles per day) I use the Backpacker's Boat *and* paddles, Bivouac Bag Inflator, *lightweight waders and* Air Pillow. *This weighs about 6¹/₂ pounds and eliminates the need for a tent entirely. I can make it for 2 weeks or more with this lightweight set up. The Fishing Float is the better fishing rig, but lightweight counts too.*

The way to use either unit is to cast to the shoreline and retrieve down the bank. Sinking line in bright daylight hours, floating line at darker times. Nymphs and minnow imitations for bright sunlight, floating moth and minnow imitations at darker times.

The anchor set up helps if its windy. Anchor and fish the rough shoreline, casting with the wind. The fish will come to you; so you don't have to move. My special reel is ideal because of the long casts possible: 100 to 200 feet are reachable with the wind and no tangles.

PACIFIC NORTHWEST

From Jim Green and Wray Lertora

As far as spinning lures are concerned, there are a good many that are popular, but I've found that ¹/₁₆ and ¹/₈ ounce gray, brown, black and white Rooster Tails work very well for trout. No. "0" and "1" Mepps Aglia spinners are also very effective. Fishing with small spoons in larger streams and lakes is also very productive. My favorite spoons for this type of fishing are the S-1 Hopkins, the ¹/₈ ounce Kastmaster, and ¹/₄ Lil Structure Spoon from Saddleback Tackle.

Jim has several favorite trout fly patterns for the Northwest. Dry flies

117

include the Renegade, Salmon Candy and the McKenzie Stone.

Some productive wet flies and nymphs are the Carey Special, Dragon Fly Nymph, Hutchinson's Damselfly Nymph and the TDC Nymph. The White Marabou Muddler and the Standard Muddler Minnow, Candlelite, and the Skykomish Sunrise are 'favorite' streamers.

IDAHO

From Bill Mason

FLIES

Adams	#14—20
Speckled Spinner	#16
Gray Nymph	#14

Adams in larger size, as well as the Speckled Spinner, will imitate the Calibeatis *genus of mayflies that far and above is predominate in lakes. The smaller Adams can imitate surface midge activity. Gray Nymph will imitate Calibeatis Nymph.*

Gray Midge Pupa	#16—18
Black Midge Pupa	#16—18
Hemingway Caddis	#12—18
(Henryville type)	
Mason Brown Caddis Pupa	#12—16
Mason Olive Caddis Pupa	#12—16
Olive Damsel Nymph	#10
Brown Damsel Nymph	#10
Olive Troth Shrimp	#12—16
Otter Shrimp	#10—16

LURES

Gold and silver Mepps	$^{1}/_{8}$—$^{1}/_{4}$ oz.
Panther Martins	$^{1}/_{4}$ oz.
Daredevils	$^{3}/_{8}$ oz.
Eddie Pope's Hotshot	$^{3}/_{8}$ oz.

WEST YELLOWSTONE

From Bud Lilly

NYMPHS

Otter Nymph: weighted #10, 12, 14
Black Wooly Worm: 8, 10, 12
Olive Wooly Worm: long shank #6, 8, 10
Zug Bug: #8, 10, 12

STREAMERS

Muddler Minnow: weighted #4, 6, 8
Light Spruce: #4, 6, 8
Hornberg Special: 8, 10

WET FLIED

Gray Hackle Peacock: #12
Lady Mith: #10
Ginger Quill: #12

DRY FLIES

Adams: #14, 16
Black Gnat: #16, 18
Goofus Bug: #14, 16, 18
Grasshopper: #10, 12, 14
Pheasant Caddis: #12, 14
Blue Dun: #16, 18

SPINNING LURES: Mepps #1 and 2 Gold; Jake's Spin-a-lure Gold; Thomas Cyclone Gold, $^1/_4$ ounce; Thomas Cyclone Copper, $^1/_4$ ounce; Kastmaster gold, $^1/_4$ or $^3/_8$ ounce.

WEST COAST

From Rex Gerlach

In the Pacific Northwest area, backpacking is done at moderate elevations up to say, around 3700 feet, as well as in the higher elevations. In parts of Washington's Columbia basin, it is done at low elevation down through sand dune country; so in that area you really have quite a range of flies that may be needed, all the way from effective dragon and damselfly nymph patterns for low elevation seepage lakes, on up through a wide range of mayfly and chironomid imitators used at higher elevations. My recommendation to a backpacker in the Pacific Northwest and in California would be a very well-rounded fly box, including dry flies and nymphs. To imitate mayflies, midges, fresh-water shrimps, damselfly nymphs, dragonfly nymphs, the Ogara Shrimp is one of the better shrimp imitators that I've tried. You'll find that dressing in Sid Gordon's book, How to Fish from Top to Bottom. It's all muskrat-dubbed fur held together with gold wire.

Virtually every Pacific angler has his own dragonfly nymph imitators; most of them work quite well. A good generic pattern that works when both dragonfly and damselfly nymphs are active, is a simple shaped body of olive-colored chenille and a short collar of greenish-brown pheasant rump tied with a single feather. This is usually tied on a 3 to 4× long 8 through 4 sized hooks.

The Royal Coachman Bucktail is a staple at virtually all elevations throughout the Western region from Montana west to Washington down Oregon and California. It's used all the way from size 4 down to size 18—very effective. Any western backpacker should have a few Black Drake Mayfly imitators, size 14, as well as some cream-colored mayflies, ranging down as small as size 22. A small grey sedge in size 22 to 28 is also used.

Insofar as spinning lures go, any good popular lure in the $1/32$ to $1/4$ ounce weight range is effective. I like the little, tiny Mepps and the Panther Martins, as well as any.

SIERRAS

From Doug McKinsey

DRY FLIES: Adams sizes 12-18; Humpy Yellow sizes 10-16; Calif. Mosquito sizes 12-16; Light Cahill sizes 12-18; Elk Hair Caddis (Troth Caddis) sizes 10-18; Royal Wulff 8-14;
WET FLIES: Western Coachman, sizes 10-14; Timberline Emerger sizes 12-16.
NYMPHS: Gold Ribbed Hairs Ear, sizes 10-14; Black A.P. Nymph sizes 10-16; Golden Stonefly sizes 8-12; Brown Stonefly sizes 4-10 (popular stonefly nymphs like the Whitlock series)
STREAMERS: Muddler Minnow sizes 6-12; Whitlock Sculpin sizes 1-8; Marabou Muddler sizes 6-12; Little Brown Trout sizes 6-10; Little Rainbow Trout sizes 6-10.

REGIONAL CONTRIBUTORS

Lefty Kreh is the author of *Fly Casting with Lefty Kreh, Fly Fishing in Salt Water* and co-author with Mark Sosin of *Practical Fishing Knots*. Skilled in all facets of angling, he is very familiar with the mountain regions of the Southeast.

Bob Leeman writes, hosts a television show, and operates a tackle shop in his native state of Maine.

Dick Surette formerly operated a tackle shop in New Hampshire and is currently Editor-Publisher of the specialty magazine *Fly Tyer*.

Lionel Atwill is a near neighbor in Dorset, Vermont. He formerly edited *Adirondack Life* and has been a contributing editor of *Backpacker* magazine. Currently he is Eastern Field Editor of *Outdoor Life*.

John Merwin is another near neighbor and former managing editor of *Fly Fisherman* magazine. Presently he is Editor-Publisher of *Rod and Reel* magazine. He recently edited the valuable book *Stillwater Trout* (Doubleday) which is a "must read" compilation of information and technique for the increasingly popular quest for trout in ponds and lakes.

Dick Pobst is an innovative angler and author of *Fish The Impossible Places*, the treatise on the Keel Fly concept. He operates a tackle shop in Ada, Michigan.

Charles Loughridge is a skilled angler who helped introduce me to several Colorado waters. He's fished, guided, and operated a tackle shop in Colorado until his recent move to St. Anthony, Idaho.

Del Canty has specialized in angling for large trout from his home base in Leadville, Colorado. He's also spent portions of each season backpacking and fishing in the Wind River areas.

Bill Mason is a skilled and knowledgeable Idaho angler involved with a variety of programs of interest to the angler-packer from his Sun Valley base of operations.

Bud Lilly has fished, guided, and operated a tackle shop for several years in one of the great fishing-backpacking areas of the country: West Yellowstone, Montana.

Doug McKinsey is familiar with Sierra requirements from his own experience and affiliation with Buz's Fly and Tackle Shop in Visalia, California.

Jim Green is a noted angler, caster and rod designer from Fenwick who combined with Wray Lertora of Fenwick for valuable Pacific Northwest information.

Rex Gerlach has written extensively for newspapers, magazines and books, including *Fly Fishing The Lakes*. Currently he is associated with Daiwa Corporation in Gardena, California.

Credits

Page 1 , Arthur C. Neumann
Page 21, 25-29, 31 , Bill Cairns
Page 36, Lefty Kreh
Page 40, 43, 46 , Bill Cairns
Page 47 , Dick Pobst
Page 50, 51, 53 (top) , Bill
    Cairns
Page 53 (bottom) , Dick Pobst
Page 55 , Bill Cairns
Page 58 , The Orvis Co., Inc.
Page 59-64, 67-69, 71, 72, 76,
    77 , Bill Cairns
Page 81 , Chart: Courtesy of The
    Orvis Co., Inc.
Page 82 , Taper Charts:
    Courtesy of the Cortland
    Line Co.
Page 85 , Knot Diagrams: Cour-
    tesy of The Orvis Co., Inc.
Page 87 , Bill Cairns
Page 89 , The Orvis Co., Inc.
Page 93 , Bill Cairns
Page 94 , Cortland Line Co.
Page 98 , Bill Cairns
Page 101 , Royal Red Ball
Page 109 , Bill Cairns

Outdoor Books from Stone Wall Press

Vanishing Fishes of North America by Dr. R. Dana Ono, Dr. James D. Williams, and Anne Wagner. Color art by Aleta Pahl, and rare photographs. 272 pages, color plates, illustrations, hardcover $29.95

> As we selfishly alter our water systems, pollute our waters, and introduce exotic fishes to our waters, we not only force species of fish to the brink of extinction, we threaten our own survival as well. This book focuses on fourteen North American ecosystems and more than sixty fishes on the very brink of extinction. Case histories are included with accompanying rare photography and color art by award-winning wildlife artist Aleta Pahl. This would be a treasured gift for any serious fisherman!

Backwoods Ethics
Environmental Concerns for Hikers and Campers by Laura and Guy Waterman. 192 pages, illustrations, index, paper-bound, $9.95

> Noted outdoor magazine columnists shed light on sensitive environmental issues with neighborly warmth and humor. "Outdoorsmen and conservationists concerned about the delicate balance between the use and preservation of our wilderness areas should find this book of great value." *EnviroSouth.* A valuable look at how outdoorsmen can individually do something to prevent further abuse and erosion of the environment. Endorsed and selected by the American Hiking Society.

MOVIN' OUT: Equipment & Techniques for Hikers by Harry Roberts. 156 pages, illustrations, index, paperbound, $9.95

> A thorough introduction to backpacking by an outfitter and wilderness expert. No-nonsense wisdom is accompanied by practical money-saving advice for choosing the best clothing and equipment for your purposes—what you need and don't need. Also, how to best use that equipment you just bought. "An excellent, down-to-earth book on backpacking information!" *International Backpackers Association.*

Wild Preserves Illustrated Recipes for Over 100 Natural Jams and Jellies by Joe Freitus. 192 pages, illustrations, paperback, $9.95

> Preserving wild fruit is a simple and delicious job, but the canner must know about the fruit and its preservability before starting. Freitus discusses pectin levels, sugar content and cooking procedures. "A happy combination of plant identification information and recipes makes this book for the pockets of hunters, camera fans, hikers, followers of Euell Gibbons or just weekend wanderers. Joe Freitus has written the creative canner's bible!" *The Conservationist.*

Stalking Trout, A Serious Fisherman's Guide by Les Hill and Graeme Marshall. 170 pages, color photographs, illustrations, hardcover, $24.95

Fishing to sighted trout is probably the most heart-stopping, exciting and downright thrilling way of trout fishing known to man. This book sets out to clarify some of the mysteries of stalking and successfully fishing to large trout. These New Zealand authors also provide excellent practical information for that special trip. Breathtaking color photos included.

Swimming Flies: A Revolutionary Aproach to Successful Fly Fishing by Georges Odier. 208 pages, photographs, illustrations, hardcover, $19.95

This is a major breakthrough in the art and science of successful fresh water fly fishing! Through empirical observation, supported by an aquatic entomologist from Montana, this Colorado guide has discovered that a family of trout flies actually swims under water. Through adaptions of already popular fly patterns and by emulating the swimming fly with new equipment and techniques, Georges has uncovered a revolutionary new method of fly fishing, stream-proven in the U.S. Canada and Europe.

Where Rivers Run, a 6,000 Mile Exploration of Canada by Canoe by Gary and Joanie McGuffin. 272 pages, photographs, maps, illustrations, hard-cover, $23.95

This remarkable trans-Canadian canoeing odyssey by two young newlyweds brings out the challange and hardships of some of this country's most dangerous rivers. Complete with maps, illustrations, and beautiful color photographs, this saga has become an instant best seller in Canada.

If these books are not available through your tackle or book store, or through our distributor (Charles E. Tuttle Co., Box 410, Rutland, VT 05701), please send your check or money order for the total list price plus $2.00 shipping and handling to

STONE WALL PRESS, INC.
1241 30th Street, NW
Washington, DC 20007

TROUT UNLIMITED

YES, I believe in the goals & objectives of Trout Unlimited, a national organization, and wish to be enrolled as a member. *Enclosed please find $ _____

☐ 31   Please make me a part of TU's Conservation Action Network.

Name _____ Occupation _____

Mail Application to:

Address _____ Telephone _____

Trout Unlimited
501 Church St., NE
Vienna, VA 22180

City/State/ZIP _____

Please Indicate   ☐ $20 Regular Membership   ☐ $50–$499 Business Member
☐ New   ☐ $25 Family Membership   ☐ $100 Century Member
☐ Renewal   ☐ $10 Student Member   ☐ $500 Life Member
                   ☐ $40–$99 Sponsor

☐ Check Enclosed   ☐ VISA   ☐ MasterCard   Card Number _____ Exp. Date _____

                                        Sponsor
Chapter _____ (if applicable) _____

*All contributions over $5 are tax deductible. Make checks payable to Trout Unlimited.

TROUT UNLIMITED

YES, I believe in the goals & objectives of Trout Unlimited, a national organization, and wish to be enrolled as a member. *Enclosed please find $ _____

☐ 31   Please make me a part of TU's Conservation Action Network.

Name _____ Occupation _____

Mail Application to:

Address _____ Telephone _____

Trout Unlimited
501 Church St., NE
Vienna, VA 22180

City/State/ZIP _____

Please Indicate   ☐ $20 Regular Membership   ☐ $50–$499 Business Member
☐ New   ☐ $25 Family Membership   ☐ $100 Century Member
☐ Renewal   ☐ $10 Student Member   ☐ $500 Life Member
                   ☐ $40–$99 Sponsor

☐ Check Enclosed   ☐ VISA   ☐ MasterCard   Card Number _____ Exp. Date _____

                                        Sponsor
Chapter _____ (if applicable) _____

*All contributions over $5 are tax deductible. Make checks payable to Trout Unlimited.